CALL ME BY MY TRUE NAMES

THE COLLECTED POEMS OF

THICH NHAT HANH

WITH AN INTRODUCTION BY OCEAN VUONG

PARALLAX PRESS
BERKELEY, CALIFORNIA

Parallax Press
2236B Sixth Street
Berkeley, California 94710
www.parallax.org

Parallax Press is the publishing division of Plum Village Community of
Engaged Buddhism, Inc.

All translations by the author, with the help of Vo-Dinh Mai, Teo Savory,
Chân Không, Huong Nghiêm, Anh Huong Nguyen, Sarah Lumpkin,
and many other friends. Many of these poems have appeared previously
in Vietnamese and English publications throughout the world.

"At the Edge of the Forest" is a new poem to this edition.
The revised translation is by Sister Lang Nghiem, Sister True Dedication,
and Brother Phap Linh. The additional commentary following "Please Call
Me by My True Names" was originally published in *Peace Is Every Step*.

Cover design by Katie Eberle
Text design and composition by Happenstance-Type-O-Rama
Cover art © 2022 by Andrea Starkey
ISBN: 978-1-952692-26-0

Library of Congress Cataloging-in-Publication Data
Names: Nhất Hạnh, Thích, author. | Vuong, Ocean, 1988- writer of
  introduction.
Title: Call me by my true names : the collected poems of Thich Nhat Hanh /
  With an Introduction by Ocean Vuong.
Description: Second Edition. | Berkeley, California : Parallax Press, 2022.
Identifiers: LCCN 2022027588 (print) | LCCN 2022027589 (ebook) | ISBN
  9781952692260 (paperback) | ISBN 9781952692277 (ebook)
Classification: LCC PL4378.9.N55 A17 2022 (print) | LCC PL4378.9.N55
  (ebook) | DDC 895/.92213--dc23

2 3 4 5 / 26 25 24 23 22

CONTENTS

ULTIMATE DIMENSION

INTRODUCTION

It is no coincidence that one of modern history's most iconic teachers would use poetry as a medium for sharing and the exploring the wisdom inherent in the human condition. If we go back far enough to ancient epics like *Gilgamesh,* the *Iliad,* and *Tale of Kiều,* works that have been credited to influencing social systems and thought still felt and implemented to this day, we discover in these texts one central bond: the enacting of the poem as a vehicle for civic engagement, not as polemic, but as robust and complex architectures wherein the role of the citizen is made capacious and vexed in relation to society. In other words, the work of poetry has always been the work of interbeing.

In the days following Thầy's continuation, I was asked by various media outlets, as a Buddhist author, to speak on this momentous occurrence in our community. But I declined—for what have I to say that Thầy's teaching has not already solidified, already made so self-evidently clear? His practice and life's work were always to prepare us for this moment and, in this way, prepare us for *us.* For our own grief in Samsara. I have always felt it wiser to do nothing than to do something without strong intention or proper conditions in place. But when Denise Nguyen, executive Director of the Thích Nhất Hạnh Foundation, reached out asking me to share directly with our community, and when I was asked to write in furtherance of this updated edition of *Call Me by My True Names,* these calls made sense to me, to speak to you as one among you.

Language and sound, as we know, are some of our oldest mediums of transmission. The root of the word "narrative" is "gnarus," Latin for knowledge. As such, all stories are first and foremost the translation of knowledge. But not only that, they are the transmission of energy. And, as Thầy taught us, energy cannot die. As a poet, this is a truth I live with every day. Because to read a text, even one composed in the seventeenth century BC, is to receive the linguistic energy of a mind working up to over four thousand years ago. In this way, to speak is to survive, and to teach is to shepherd our ideas into the future. The text is a raft we send forward for all later generations. We know this because we have all clung, are still clinging, to the raft of Thầy's and Buddha's teachings. How lucky we are, as a species, to have such a vehicle. I believe that language, despite major developments in medicine and science, is still our most advanced technology. We owe it to ourselves to commit to building new rafts for all sentient beings. Our work, as was Thầy's, is part of a long tradition of liberation that spans multiple epochs and myriad realms.

Yes, energy, and even people, do not truly die. But I must speak, too, as a lay practitioner, who does not yet possess the merit to devote to a monastic life, and must admit that my heart breaks to see Thầy's body prepared for cremation, to know his journey through death and dying, which, as the Buddha taught us, is one of the passages of suffering all sentient beings must move through. And because I am not strong enough in my practice, I watched the procession for Thầy's funeral with tears in my eyes, both for the beauty of the community he built but also for the immense sadness in my heart. I weep for myself and others who do not yet have the wisdom and merit to bear this pain well.

When my own mother was dying of cancer in November 2019, on her deathbed, she said to me, her voice weak, the heat energy already fading from her limbs, *Con ơi, giờ con đã biết nỗi đau này, con phải đi giúp người ta nghe. / My son, now that you know this sickness, you must take this knowledge to help people.* My mother, though illiterate, memorized Vietnamese Buddhist sutras and would listen to Thầy's teachings on her iPhone with regularity. I told her: Yes, I will not let this pain be experienced in vain. And since so many of us are feeling pain about Thầy's continuation, I think it is helpful to see sadness, too, as energy. May we let the sadness come and teach us how to live. Let it be the mud for the lotus, as Thầy says. Let us sit with it and let it pass through us so that it might be transformed to something like love. My mother, having learned from Thầy, knew that pain can be recycled into knowledge. Isn't that what language is for?

And I ask you now, specifically our monastic brothers and sisters, folks, and elders, as you have Xuất Gia, or "went forth," and therefore are the true pioneers of human phenomena, I ask you humbly, to seek, in your practice (as I am sure you have already done), all the ways sadness might be transformed. And we, the lay practitioners who have "remained," will follow your path. This is why monastics are, to my mind, the true embodiments of courage, are warriors more grounded and determined than anyone who has ever raised a sword: you have chosen to shave your heads and march into the vast unknown, beyond the cliff of human knowledge, while we remain here in relative safety and comfort, awaiting your discoveries, ready to go forth.

It is said that grief is actually love—but with nowhere to go. In a quest that might very well take up the remainder of my life in this form, I ask of myself and also of you, dear community: where shall we go, both within and outside us? Now that we have such a capacious raft, one that can hold so many, fortified by Thầy's teachings, there might still be sadness, yes, but there is no more fear.

Knowing you are out there, mining the answers when you sit down, when you follow your breath, when you make offerings, knowing you are just ahead of us, and that I can glimpse your bright robes along the road, like scraps of sunlight among the grey detritus, how can I ever be scared? But more so, how can I ever be lost?

I am sad, yes. And I will be so for some time. My heart aches—but despite, or perhaps because of that, I have found you. And in you I have found myself.

That is the narrative, that is the knowledge. And poems, these included, make it possible.

Yours, in hope and word,

OCEAN VUONG
(PHÁP DANH: ĐỨC HẢI)
Northampton, Massachusetts
May 2022

If you touch deeply the historical dimension,
you find yourself in the ultimate dimension.
If you touch the ultimate dimension,
you have not left the historical dimension—

HISTORICAL
DIMENSION

MESSAGE

Life has left her footprints on my forehead.
But I have become a child again this morning.
The smile, seen through leaves and flowers,
is back to smooth away the wrinkles,
as the rains wipe away footprints on the beach.
Again a cycle of birth and death begins.

I walk on thorns, but firmly, as among flowers.
I keep my head high.
Rhymes bloom among the sounds of bombs and mortars.
The tears I shed yesterday have become rain.
I feel calm hearing its sound on the thatched roof.
Childhood, my birthland, is calling me,
and the rains melt my despair.

I am still here alive, able to smile quietly.
O sweet fruit brought forth by the tree of suffering!
Carrying the dead body of my brother,
I go across the rice field in the darkness.
Earth will keep you tight within her arms, my dear,
so that tomorrow you will be reborn as flowers,
those flowers smiling quietly in the morning field.
This moment you weep no more, my dear.
We have gone through too deep a night.

This morning,
I kneel down on the grass,
when I notice your presence.
Flowers that carry the marvelous smile of ineffability
speak to me in silence.

The message,
the message of love
and understanding,
has indeed come to us.

*Written in 1964 in Saigon. Printed in 1966 by the Fellowship of
Reconciliation as a Christmas card.*

OUR GREEN GARDEN

Fires spring up at all ten points of the universe.
A furious, acrid wind sweeps them toward us from all sides.
Aloof and beautiful, the mountains and rivers abide.

All around, the horizon burns with the color of death.
As for me, yes, I am still alive,
but my body and soul writhe as if they too had been set on fire.
My parched eyes can shed no more tears.

Where are you going this evening, dear brother, in what
    direction?
The rattle of gunfire is close at hand.
In her breast, the heart of our mother shrivels and
fades like a dying flower.
She bows her head,
her smooth black hair now threaded with white.
How many nights has she crouched, wide awake,
alone with her lantern, praying for the storm to end?

Dearest brother, I know it is *you* who will shoot me tonight,
piercing our mother's heart with a wound that can never heal.
O terrible winds that blow from the ends of the Earth,
hurling down our houses and blasting our fertile fields!

I say farewell to the blazing, blackening place where I was
    born.
Here is my breast! Aim your gun at it, brother, shoot!
I offer my body, the body our mother bore and nurtured.
Destroy it if you wish.

Destroy it in the name of your dream—
that dream in whose name you kill.

Can you hear me invoke the darkness,
"When will the suffering end?
O darkness, in whose name do you destroy?"

Come back, dear brother, and kneel at our mother's knee.
Don't sacrifice our green garden
to the ragged flames that have been carried into the front yard
by wild winds from far away.

Here is my breast. Aim your gun at it, brother, shoot!
Destroy me if you wish
and build from my carrion
whatever it is you are dreaming of.

Who will be left to celebrate a victory made of blood and fire?

*This antiwar poem was written around 1964–1965 and printed in the
Buddhist weekly Hai Triêu Am (The Sound of the Rising Tide).*

MUDRA

Don't listen to the poet.
In his morning coffee, there is a teardrop.

Don't listen to me.
Please don't.
In my morning coffee, there is a drop of blood.
Don't scold me, brother,
because I cannot swallow liquids.
The air in my lungs is frozen.

He said, "Let me weep through your eyes
because I no longer have eyes.
Let me walk on your feet,
because I have no feet."
With my hands
I am touching your nightmare.
He said, "I have been saved.
I need no more salvation."
Salvation is for us.

My hand on the table,
the cosmos remains silent.
The great ocean has never calmed her sobbing.
The five mountains maintain
the original positions of Sky and Earth.

Far above the Milky Way,
the secrets of the universe reveal themselves.
Yet my right hand is on the table—
waiting for humankind to wake up.

No, my hand will never turn over on this table
like the half-shell
balancing on the shore,
like the corpse of a man struck down by a bullet.
Mountain and river are overthrown.
Celestial bodies are out,
and the great ocean ceases its everlasting murmur.

My hand is still on the table,
and the five mountains
still dominate.
The secret has not been revealed.
The celestial bodies go on conversing with each other.
My hand is still on the table,
waiting for the moment
to reverse the balance of Sky and Earth—
my hand,
this small hand,
is like a mountain.

A mudra is a hand gesture used in meditation to evoke a particular state. In 1967, I read this poem and "Peace" at Town Hall in New York City with Arthur Miller, Robert Lowell, Daniel Berrigan, and twenty other poets. The phrase, "Don't listen to the poet" is a way to say that he is suffering a lot, and, if you listen to him, you will suffer too. "Don't scold me, brother, because I cannot swallow liquids. The air in my lungs is frozen." This means you cannot enjoy your coffee because there is blood in it. The person who is dead tells me that he wants to borrow my eyes in order to weep, because he does not have any eyes. The veteran who cannot walk says, "Let me walk on your feet, because I have no feet." One year later, speaking at an international conference in Montréal, I pleaded, "Liberate us from your liberation." The mudra in this poem is formed like this: I put my hand on the table in the shape of a mountain. We have to be very firm, very concentrated, to maintain stability; otherwise we will lose our balance.

EXPERIENCE

I have come to be with you,
to weep with you
for our ravaged land
and broken lives.
We are left with only grief and pain,
but take my hands
and hold them, hold them.
I want to say
only simple words.
Have courage. We must have courage,
if only for the children,
if only for tomorrow.

During the month after the flood,
the young man received only two pounds of rice
from the emergency aid.
Tonight he is eating areca tops and rotten corn.
And he is one of so many children,
jaundiced, with bloated faces.

He had dysentery for a week
with no medicine
and no hope.

The flood carried off
his father,
his mother,
and his brother.
This innocent child's brow
wears no mourning band.

But from the scorched and gutted fields,
a sickly ray of sun
comes to envelop my soul
in its ghoulish sheet.

Please come here
and witness
the ordeal of all the dear ones
who survived the flood of the Year of the Dragon.

Take this bleeding child in your arms.
She is the only member of her household
whose misfortune was to survive.

A young father
whose wife and four children died
stares, day and night, into empty space.
He sometimes laughs
a tear-choked laugh.

Please come and see
his white-haired elder,
left alone for days on a barren, weedy patch of land.
He kneels before a startled boy
who offers him some rice.
He is kneeling in love
while the boy weeps,
"O grandfather, don't kneel in front of me.
I am the age of your grandson."

The message of love has been transmitted.
Again, I put my faith in tomorrow.

Her husband is dead,
her children dead,
her land ruined,
her hearth cold.
There is no spark to light a fire,
for death is here
on a patch of earth sucked dry.

Nothing remains,
for the last one left,
not even her resignation.

She curses aloud her existence.
"How fortunate," she says,
"those families who died together."

I tell her, "We are not alone.
There are others,
and we must help still their cries
on this endless road.
Let us walk on with our heads bent."

The villager looks me over.
Agonized yet fearless,
he answers,
"I hate both sides.
I follow neither.
I only want to go
where they will let me live
and help me live."
O life! What misery!

On this high place by the Thu Bon River,
I cut my finger
and watch the blood drip
and mix with the water.
O be at rest,
you who are lost.
O be at peace!

To you who have drowned, I speak,
and to you who have survived,
and to the river—
having heard all space reverberate
with the infants' screams.
Tonight
I've come to stand midway
between these sheer mountains,
and to watch them bend over the river,
and to listen
to their eternal tales.

Here is the impermanent
and yet continuously flowing world.
Let us stand together for future generations.

Each tiny bodhisattva,
with bowed head and hidden tears,
student's ink still on her hands,
holds a shovel or a mattock
and throws up earth for a bridge
or for burying the bloated dead.

Under palm-leaf hats,
brown-clothed and barefoot,
are they not Quan Yin in all her glory,
her charity, her fearlessness?

The small, bare feet walk over stones,
the sharp stones of pain and grief.
The bare feet enter shacks
built hastily on ash,
that they may approach the living
who have reached the limits of their lives.

While I watch their hands,
as gentle as heavenly silk,
outstretched to infants,
the crying stops,
and the mother's eyes,
staring at cans of milk,
glow like precious stones.

And still I sit
before the Gates of Heaven
tightly shut
with bowed head, waiting.

In the old garden, I wonder,
could one feel the fragrance
of areca blossoms?

O here,
why is there such silence?—
such silence,

when even the birds of our stricken land
have vanished.
O speak out now,
speak audibly again,
so hearing you in far corners
our birds will return;
our waters be like jewels again;
our land like brocade.

O sing,
sing aloud
so True Being may follow the Word.

I wrote this poem in 1964 following a rescue operation. We went in several boats up the Thu Bon River to bring relief to the victims of flooding and the war in the Duc Duc area of Quang Nam Province. It was very dangerous to go there. We were stopped along the way by both warring sides. When we were stopped and searched by the nationalists, I asked them, "What if we are stopped by the other side and given propaganda literature? I certainly could not refuse." "Of course, you may accept it, but when you get to the stream, drop it in." I asked, "What if I don't have time to release it before being caught by someone like you?" They did not answer.

After finishing the work, we stayed a few days with the people. The shooting was directly above our heads. One disciple of mine jumped into the water, he was so nervous. The suffering was overwhelming. I bit my finger and let a drop of blood fall into the river, saying, "This is to pray for all of you who have perished in the war and the flood."

The day we left, many young women standing on the shore tried to hand us their babies, but we knew we could not take care of them. We felt so helpless, we cried.

FOR WARMTH

I hold my face in my two hands.
No, I am not crying.
I hold my face in my two hands
to keep the loneliness warm—
two hands protecting,
two hands nourishing,
two hands preventing
my soul from leaving me
in anger.

This was written after I heard about the bombing of Ben Tre and the comment made by an American military man, "We had to destroy the town in order to save it." Betsy Rose set this poem to music in a song called "In My Two Hands."

NIGHT OF PRAYER

In that moment,
the wind was still,
the birds silent.
Seven times the Earth shook
as immortality traversed
the stream of birth and death.
The hand on the wheel
in the mudra of peace
bloomed like a flower in the night.

In that moment,
the flower of immortality opened
in the garden of birth and death—
the enlightened smiles:
words and similes.
He has come
to learn man's language.

That night in Tushita Heaven,
the gods looked down,
saw Earth, my homeland, brighter than a star,
while galaxies inclined, worshipping
till East turned rose,
and the Lumbini gardens became a soft cradle
welcoming Buddha, newly born.

Tonight, tonight
on Earth, my homeland,
men look up.
Their tear-blind eyes turn toward Tushita Heaven.

The cries of pain are everywhere,
as Mara's hand bears down in violence and hatred.

In darkness Earth, my homeland,
yearns for the miraculous event
when eternity parts its curtains,
shadows dissolve,
and Maitreya comes to my land.
The sound of being echoes again
in the singing of a child.

Tonight the moon and the stars bear witness.
Let my homeland, let Earth pray
for Vietnam—
her deaths and fires,
grief and blood—
that Vietnam will rise from her suffering
and become that soft, new cradle
for the Buddha-to-come.
Let Earth, my country, pray
that once more the flower blooms.

Tonight we hope
that our agony will bear fruit;
that birth and death will cross
the stream of immortality
and love's spring bathe ten thousand hearts;
that man will learn the language of the inexpressible.
Then the babble of a child
will teach the way.

Written in 1964 and printed in Hai Triêu Am *weekly. Music composed in Tokyo in 1968.*

RECOMMENDATION

Promise me,
promise me this day,
promise me now,
while the sun is overhead
exactly at the zenith,
promise me:

Even as they
strike you down
with a mountain of hatred and violence;
even as they step on you and crush you
like a worm,
even as they dismember and disembowel you,
remember, brother,
remember:
man is not our enemy.

The only thing worthy of you is compassion—
invincible, limitless, unconditional.
Hatred will never let you face
the beast in man.

One day, when you face this beast alone,
with your courage intact, your eyes kind,
untroubled
(even as no one sees them),
out of your smile
will bloom a flower.
And those who love you
will behold you

across ten thousand worlds of birth and dying.

Alone again,
I will go on with bent head,
knowing that love has become eternal.
On the long, rough road,
the sun and the moon
will continue to shine.

I wrote this poem in 1965 especially for the young people in the School of Youth for Social Service who risked their lives every day during the war, recommending them to prepare to die without hatred. Some had already been killed violently, and I cautioned the others against hating. Our enemy is our anger, hatred, greed, fanaticism, and discrimination against men. If you die because of violence, you must meditate on compassion in order to forgive those who kill you. When you die realizing this state of compassion, you are truly a child of the Awakened One. Even if you are dying in oppression, shame, and violence, if you can smile with forgiveness, you have great power.

Rereading the lines of this poem, I suddenly understood the passage in the Diamond Sutra *that speaks about* kshanti, *endurance or tolerance: "Your courage intact, your eyes kind, untroubled (even as no one sees them), out of your smile will bloom a flower. And those who love you will behold you across ten thousand worlds of birth and dying." If you die with compassion in mind, you are a torch lighting our path. Before burning herself, Nhat Chi Mai, one of the earliest Tiep Hien members, read this poem into a tape and left it for her parents.*

"Alone again I will go on with bent head" in order to see you, know you, remember you. Your love has become eternal. "On the long, rough road, the sun and the moon will continue to shine." When there is a mature relationship between people, there is always compassion and forgiveness. In our life, we need others to see and recognize us so that we feel supported. How much more do we need the Buddha to see us! On our path of service, there are moments of pain and loneliness, but when we know that the Buddha sees and knows us, we feel a great surge of energy and a firm determination to carry on.

The brothers of Weston Priory put this poem into beautiful music.

STRUCTURE OF SUCHNESS

Do not scold the little birds.
We need their songs.
Do not hate your own body.
It is the altar for humanity's spirit.

Your eyes contain the trichiliocosm,
and your ears have sovereignty over the birds,
the springs, the rising tide,
Beethoven, Bach, Chopin,
the cries of the baby,
and the song that lulls her to sleep.
Your hands are flowers of love
that need not be picked by anyone,
and your forehead
is the most beautiful morning of all mornings.
Do not destroy the structure of suchness within you.

The corn, the grass, and the fragrance of the night
have all spoken out for peace.
I know a bullet may strike
the heart of the little bird this morning,
the bird that is celebrating life with all its might.
The corn, the grass, the fragrance of the night,
together with the stars and the moon—
all of us are doing our best.
We are doing everything we can
to keep you alive.

RESOLUTION

You fight us
because we fight hatred,
while you feed on hatred and violence
for strength.

You curse us
because we don't give man a label
and turn a gun barrel on him.

You condemn us
because you can't use our blood
in paying off your debts of greed;
because you can't budge us
from man's side,
where we stand to protect all life.

And you murder us
just because we bow our heads
before man's love and reason;
because
we steadfastly refuse
to identify him
with the wolves.

Written during the war in the 1960s.

THOSE THAT HAVE NOT EXPLODED

I don't know,
I just do not know
why
they hurl grenades
at these young people.

Why wish to kill
those boys with still innocent brows,
those girls with ink-stained hands?

What was their crime?—
to hear the voice of compassion?
to come and live in a hamlet,
to help the villagers,
teach the children,
work in the rice paddies?

Last night when those grenades burst,
twelve young people fell
with mangled bodies and burst skin.
One girl's flesh took more than 600 metal bits of shrapnel.

This morning, two are buried.
Each waits for the sun to rise again
in our motherland.
Each longs for peace,
to be reborn as a butterfly.

We accept death and sorrow.
But listen,

brothers and sisters,
those grenades have burst
and ripped apart the sky.
Those boys and girls are gone,
leaving a trail of blood.

But there are more grenades
than those that burst last night.
There are more grenades
caught in the heart of life.
Do you hear me?
There are more that are yet to burst.

They remain
still
in the heart of man—
unknown, the time of their detonation;
unknown, when they will desecrate our land;
unknown, the time they will annihilate our people.

And still
we beg you to believe
there is no hatred in our hearts,
no rancor in our souls.
What the world needs,
what we all need
is love.

Come, hear me,
for time grows short
and danger is everywhere.
Let us take those grenades

out of our hearts,
our motherland,
humankind.
Let us stand.
Let us stand
side by side.

This poem was written in 1966 after an attack on the School of Youth for Social Service by a group of unknown men with grenades and guns.

LET ME GIVE BACK TO OUR MOTHERLAND

Last night four of my brothers died.
One was Tho.
One was Tuan.
One was Hy.
One was Lanh.
Let this be known to you,
brothers, sisters, my people, my motherland.

Four young men heard my appeal
and went out to the hamlets,
sowing trust and love
so that peace might reappear.

Their flesh is mine.
Their blood is mine.
My flesh is crushed.
My blood is dried.
At midnight they were dragged
barefoot, bareheaded,
to the riverside,
pushed to their knees, and shot.
(And I was shot down on the riverbank.)

In your presence, fellow countrymen,
brothers and sisters,
let me return the flesh of my brothers to our motherland.
Let me return the blood of my brothers to our motherland—
this chaste blood and pure flesh that never soiled our name.

Let me return their hands to humanity,
hands that did not destroy.
Let me give back their hearts to humanity,
hearts that bore no hatred.

As for the skin of their bodies,
let me give this back to you, fellow countrymen,
the skin of four who never cooked an animal's flesh
in its own skin.

Use, please use the skin of my brothers
to mend those open wounds in our people's flesh,
that immense body
that swoons in agony.

I was in Paris when I heard about the assassination of four students of the School of Youth for Social Service, a school I had helped start. I cried. A friend named Mr. Windmiller said, "Thây, you should not cry. You are a general leading an army of nonviolent soldiers. It is natural that you suffer casualties." I said, "No, I am not a general. I am just a human being. It is I who summoned them for service, and now they have lost their lives. I need to cry."

THE WITNESS REMAINS

Flarebombs bloom on the dark sky.
A child claps his hands and laughs.
I hear the sound of guns,
and the laughter dies.

But the witness
remains.

Flarebombs are to detect the presence of enemies. When you are dominated by fear, anyone can be seen as an enemy, even a little child. The witness is you. And me.

PEACE

They woke me this morning
to tell me my brother had been killed in battle.
Yet in the garden
a new rose, with moist petals uncurling,
blooms on the bush.
And I am alive,
still breathing the fragrance of roses and dung,
eating, praying, and sleeping.
When can I break my long silence?
When can I speak the unuttered words that are choking me?

This antiwar poem was written in Vietnam in 1964, when to pronounce the word "peace" meant you were "communist," helping the communists, or just defeatist. When Pham Duy, a well-known musician, put this poem to music, he used the title "A Dream."

FLAMES OF PRAYER

Early morning.
The sun is shining.
Oh cosmos, how I yearn to embrace you in my arms.
Birds are singing.
A woman selling breakfast passes by the bamboo grove.
O homeland, how I yearn to embrace you in my arms.
People are gathering at the marketplace.
O world, how I yearn to embrace you in my arms.
Only twenty more hours, yet already I am not here.
I will give myself to Fire.
The sun is shining. O homeland, O world, O cosmos!

All is beauty unsurpassed.
Separation will be unbearable,
my love immeasurable.
So many memories—
yet I will not be able to take with me
even a single leaf or pebble.
Each leaf is so precious; each pebble oh so precious.

Waking up early, I have slept soundly,
like an innocent child with no worries.
My hands, is it your duty to call Fire home this morning?
My hands caress my cheeks.
My hands, you are loyal friends,
hands for handing out candies and cookies,
hands that are smudged with ink and chalk,
hands for weaving silk,
hands for smoothing the heads of orphans.

Waking up early, oh how I want to live forever!
Each rose-colored morning,
each new morning begins a full day
like a blank sheet of paper
ready to be filled with meaning.
Why is the cosmos so beautiful today?
Is it because I am about to die?
Or because I have opened my eyes?
Oh the many stars, so far away!

Waking up early,
aware of my face, my hands,
and this small basin of water.
How I yearn to swim in that crystal clear water,
to be a tiny fish!

Waking up early,
my windows open to the pristine air,
how I yearn to fly up in it,
to be a little bird!

Waking up early,
I see a group of schoolchildren crossing the street
chirping like birds.
Walk forth, my little brothers and sisters.
Walk forth toward the peaceful, safe horizon
where there is no suffering, no killing!
Here I plunge into the pit of bloody fire.
Go forth quickly, my dear ones.
Here the rocky hills, the mountains and forests,
are all doing their best to stop the bloody fire!

Far ahead, an elder sister or brother will be waiting for you.
Your classroom will be visited
by a wandering bird or butterfly.
Your classroom will be pervaded
by the delicious, soft fragrance of a rose vine
climbing up the windowsill.
Cookies and candies will be passed under the tables.
Elder brother knows, but he still smiles.
Elder sister knows but pretends not to.
The writing assignment is being read in the southern dialect.
Mistakes with accents count only half a point.
I adore these silken-haired heads and bright eyes—
even the ink smears on the shirts and faces,
and the runny noses.

The streets are crowded with people.
What are you thinking of, Aunt?
What are you thinking of, Uncle?
What are you worrying about, Elder Brother?
What are you worrying about, Elder Sister?
Each one has a different worry,
each person a particular situation.
Everyone is going about doing their own morning errands.
I walk alone,
my feet on the ground,
but I feel I am walking on air.
I am still here, but already I have gone.

Twenty hours left.
I did not share with anyone my deepest thoughts.
I am not lonely.

O friends, O human race,
O Brothers and Sisters,
I love this Earth of ours,
tears flowing down my face.
I bend my head and wipe them away.
I smile, chastising myself.
I feel ashamed because I still love.
I am still attached, and I want to stay.
Alone, I go.

O friends, please let me go.
Don't be angry.
Please don't come too close.
Keep your distance so I can fulfill my vow.
I yearn to embrace each of you,
young and old, and to have a good cry.
But that would ruin everything.
Our tears would erode
all the determination I have mustered.
Forgive me, my friends.
Forgive me, my dear Mother and Father.
Forgive me, my darling brothers and sisters.

Remember the story of the river.
Let me be the boatman,
Let me hear the blue waves talking each morning.
Let me see Ong Lanh Bridge,
the small boats carrying bright red clay pots and pans,
others carrying vats of fish sauce.
I see the women selling areca nuts,
their lips red from chewing betel,

their hair covered with striped cloths.
Our homeland is beautiful, oh so beautiful.
There is the temple, the bamboo grove,
the areca garden, the hedge of betel,
and the familiar river port.
I want to turn back.
But even if I turn back, I cannot find my homeland!

I am touching the soil of my homeland with each step.
The soil of my homeland has been devastated
by bombs and gunfire.
Here is a prayer for those green gardens,
with bamboo and plum blossoms,
with cactus plants in the front courtyards.
Joining my palms,
I accept the flames as a prayer.
Allow me to see the houses for the last time.
Allow me to see the sky, the water, the trees for the last time.
Allow me to see the stars and the moon.
Allow me to see the people—
aunts, uncles, brothers, and sisters,
young and old.
Let me see them laughing and talking.
I embrace all in the small circle of my two arms.
I have seen you, my fellow brothers and sisters.
I am going, but I am still here.
Tomorrow as the sun rises,
my poetry will reach my beloved ones.

*Written in 1966, after I heard that Nhat Chi Mai, one of the first six people
ordained as core members of the Order of Interbeing, had immolated herself
for peace and reconciliation at Tu Nghiêm Pagoda in Saigon.*

MORNING OF PEACE

Treading the path that leads to the moon,
I look back and can't stop marveling.
I see a bubble of water on the immense ocean of space.
It is the Earth, our green planet,
her sumptuous beauty sparkling and proud,
yet oh so fragile.
In her, I discover myself.

Walking mindfully on the earth,
a grassy path,
my feet make the promise
to embrace the early morning
and touch the peace of the present moment.

Autumn leaves fall and cover the path,
unrolling a carpet of walking meditation.
A shy squirrel, hiding behind the oak tree,
looks at me, surprised,
then dashes to the top of the tree
and disappears behind a cluster of leaves.

I see a clear stream
flowing between cracks in the rocks,
its water laughing,
while the trees whistle.
Together we celebrate a morning of peace.

At the same time,
I see places of deep suffering
where men imprison men,

and make each other suffer—
the waves of discrimination, hatred, and greed,
inevitable causes of catastrophe,
crash upon the earth.
Chicks of the same hen
wear different colors in order to fight with each other.
Heartrending cries declare the horrors of war.

Brothers and sisters,
the beautiful Earth is us.
I embrace her and hold her tenderly against my chest.
Breathing together in the same rhythm
we restore our calm, our peace.
Let us accept ourselves
so we may accept one another.
Let us share the vision and make it possible
for Great Love to arise.

THE NEW HAMLET

This morning I have no matches,
and my fireplace is cold
like a damp, autumn day.
My painting is half-finished.
I go to a neighbor to ask for some fire.
(Do you remember as little boys,
we used to do this?)

You ask me what I will do if our neighbor has no fire left.
I answer, "We'll go singing together."
I remember what Mother told me,
and we'll ask you to come along to the new hamlet.
Please don't forget to sing.
I am sure someone in our hamlet still has fire.
I ask all of you
to hold up your hands
and tell me the truth.
"Do you believe, as I do,
that someone in our hamlet
is keeping the fire alive?"

I know of poor households
where a fire is always kept burning
with rice husks in the fireplace.
I remember what Mother told me.
I'll not disturb the good hearth.
I am only gently placing
onto the burning husks
a handful of straw

and waiting patiently until the smoke rises.
Then with a gentle breath, I revive the flame.

You, my brother, are back today from a long voyage.
Feel the warmth in your heart
while contemplating the light smoke covering our thatch
    house.
Please come to our hamlet.
We are waiting for you.
Our sister has been keeping the fire alive
in the ancient fireplace.

Your boat follows the stream
without hesitation
under the protecting light of the stars.

Your boat continues to come.
Even as the mist is falling,
there is no need to worry,
because you know
the love today
is enough
to provide warmth for tomorrow.

There is a good fire in my home now.
Please come for a visit.
For many thousands of years,
someone has tried to build a bridge to connect the two sides.
My painting has just been completed.
The colors are still fresh.

We want to show it to you.
The fire crackles joyfully.
We will bring in a few more candles.

This poem was written for the workers of the School of Youth for Social Service. There were no matches in the old time. You had to keep the fire alive in your kitchen. If there was no fire, you could not do any cooking. You had to go to the house of a neighbor to ask for some fire.

A PRAYER FOR PEACE

In beauty, sitting on a lotus flower,
is Lord Buddha, quiet and solid.
Your humble disciple,
calm and pure of heart,
forms a lotus flower with his hands,
faces you with deep respect,
and offers this heartfelt prayer:

Homage to all Buddhas in the ten directions.
Please have compassion for our suffering.
Our land has been at war for two decades.
Divided, it is a land of tears
and blood and bones of young and old.
Mothers weep till their tears are dry
while sons on distant fields decay.
Its beauty torn apart,
only blood and tears now flow.
Brothers killing brothers
for promises from outsiders.

Homage to all Buddhas in the ten directions.
Because of your love for all people,
have compassion on us.
Help us remember we are just one family,
North and South.
Help us rekindle our compassion and brotherhood,
and transform our separate interests
into loving acceptance for all.
May your compassion help us overcome our hatred.
May Avalokiteshvara Bodhisattva's love

help the flowers bloom again in the soil of our country.
Humbly, we open our hearts to you,
so you may help us transform our karma
and water the flowers of our spirits.
With your deep understanding,
help our hearts grow light.

Homage to Shakyamuni Buddha
whose great vows and compassion inspire us.
I am determined to cultivate only thoughts
that increase trust and love,
to use my hands to perform only deeds
that build community,
to speak only words of harmony and aid.

May the merit of this prayer
be transformed into peace in Vietnam.
May each of us realize this,
our deep aspiration.

This prayer was used throughout South Vietnam in 1965 in the "Don't Shoot Your Own Brother" campaign to rouse the willingness to work for peace. During meetings of young people, we chanted this poem, uniting our hearts and our efforts to continue to work for peace. Most of us were Buddhists. This chant aims at reconciliation and stopping the war. It was a very powerful way of working for communication. This is something we can share with Western friends.

THAT IS THE ONLY MIND

These ramparts of yours—
who has promised to build them for you?—
this morning suddenly
we find ourselves
floating on the ocean
amid winds and waves.

Suffering itself builds the last shelter
in which
you will spend
the cruelest of nights.

Do repeat to me what I have promised
(it has been a long time),
so that I will be present on that day to serve as your witness.

The arrows that struck me—I still bear them
in the flesh of my body.
They have not been returned.
Take good care of your own garden, brother.
I am a bird and, like other birds,
will only look for fresh water and good seeds.
We will be back in your garden.

Be the monarch oyour life
and sign the decree
to exile suffering
and call back from all points of the universe
the power of birds and flowers,

the vitality of youth.
The whole universe will smile
when your eyes smile.

This poem was written in 1960 in the small Bamboo Grove Temple in Gia Dinh, where my hut had a dirt floor. I wrote this for young monks and nuns, confirming my love and support. I knew they suffered so much in the situation of war.

CONDEMNATION

Listen to this:
yesterday six Vietcong came through my village,
and because of this, the village was bombed.
Every soul was killed.
When I returned to the village the next day,
there was nothing but clouds of dust—
the pagoda without roof or altar,
only the foundations of houses,
the bamboo thickets burned away.

Here in the presence of the undisturbed stars,
in the invisible presence of all people still alive on Earth,
let me raise my voice to denounce this dreadful war,
this murder of brothers by brothers!

Whoever is listening, be my witness:
I cannot accept this war.
I never could, I never will.
I must say this a thousand times before I am killed.

I am like the bird who dies for the sake of its mate,
dripping blood from its broken beak and crying out,
"Beware! Turn around and face your real enemies—
ambition, violence, hatred, and greed."

Humans are not our enemies—even those called "Vietcong."
If we kill our brothers and sisters, what will we have left?
With whom then shall we live?

This antiwar poem was written in 1964 and printed in the Buddhist weekly Hai Triêu Am (The Sound of the Rising Tide), *circulation 50,000. I earned the title "antiwar poet" and was denounced as a pro-communist propagandist. The following song, "Our Enemy" (Ke Thu Ta), written by Pham Duy, was based on the last three lines of this poem:*

> *Our enemy wears the colors of an ideology.*
> *Our enemy wears the label of liberty.*
> *Our enemy carries a fancy appearance.*
> *Our enemy carries a big basket full of words.*
> *Our enemy is not men.*
> *If we kill men, with whom shall we live?*

THE SUN OF THE FUTURE

Sitting in a wet trench
a whole afternoon,
I hold my gun down
and wait for Victor,
Victor Charlie,
the yellow-skinned Vietcong.

How sorrowful is the cry of the monkey
in this Asian mountain.
How sorrowful is this country called Vietnam.
How do these forests and mountains differ
from the forests and mountains of Africa?

My gun, barking and spitting fire,
has the eyes of Victor Charlie—
his eyes,
whether black skin or yellow skin,
what do the eyes say?—
his eyes, the sorrow of Asia.
I have heard somewhere a poet
expressing the sorrow of Africa.
It doesn't matter whether he is black or white.
Why do I have to hate you,
Victor Charlie?

Our money has been flowing into Vietnam
while my poor, black brothers
bear the burden of racism and discrimination.
Detroit, Selma, Chicago, Birmingham, Watts
are already engaged in the struggle.

My brothers and sisters have started to leave
the land of suffering.

We have taken a stand—
thirty billion dollars
for the war in 1967.
Three million dollars
for each hour of the war—
my wife and children in Chicago,
still caught in the net of poverty.
Two billion dollars for each month of the war,
more than the yearly budget to help the poor
in our country, the great America.
To support half a million immigrant families,
education,
children's programs,
housing,
and health care,
to meet the yearly budget for all of that,
we only need to stop the war for eight hours.

Why are we in Vietnam,
the forests and mountains of Asia?

Victor Charlie,
when did we sow the first seed of hatred and anger?
This is not what we meant to do!
They hid the truth from us.
They did not tell us the limits.
The sun of the future
is hidden
behind the forests and mountains.

At the foot of the Asian continent,
the Earth is trembling.
And she is trembling
under the African continent as well.

Written in 1967.

FLESH AND SKIN, BRICKS AND TILES

The bombers are gone.
Beneath a still sun,
in the dying light of noon,
our ancient land stirs again.

The curved temple roof
is burnt out, crumpled.
But Lord Buddha sits,
his gilt all smeared,
smiling ineffably at bricks and stones.

The quiet dusk
sends up a flute song
as from my soul.
Our schoolchildren
had sought shelter
in that temple
where clouds now hover.

Now they are gone,
gone, like those with heads of black and shiny hair,
for they took the wounded away,
and the dead will be buried tomorrow
in the cemetery
at the road's end.

O homeland,
O Sisters and Brothers,
your teeth are clenched.

Still today,
you bear your pain in silence.
What else can you do?
Where else can you go?
Even the sea is too shallow
for your sorrow.

O Sisters and Brothers,
what will you do
with these bullets and steel,
broken and burst in you?
O flesh and skin,
bricks and tiles.

Our past is here
in the twentieth century.
Remember, remember.
Is it true that this child,
raised on potatoes and manioc roots
of our poor land;
that this child
born after the Geneva Peace Accords;
this child
whose laughter once resounded
across spring fields
whenever the evening bell was struck in the temple;
this child—
is it true
this child has been cruelly stripped of his right
to become a man?

I still remember this scene vividly. After the Buddhist temple was bombed, there was nothing left except the statue of Lord Buddha in the main shrine, still sitting quietly and smiling. Many of the children who were taking lessons in reading and writing in the temple during the bombing were killed or wounded.

THE LONELY WATCHTOWER

High
on top
of the spiked heel
of the joy-woman's shoe,
you build your watchtower—
your loopholes open
on the shabbily thatched roofs;
your loopholes open
on the withered gardens
and burnt-out paddies,
where at night
our souls come back
and dance
in silence.

At noon,
you throw down
your empty sardine cans,
your empty beer cans,
your empty Coke bottles,
your cigarette butts.

In the afternoon,
you aim your guns' black barrels
toward the body,
the destitute body
of your own motherland.

And when evening descends,
you chase solitude away

by shooting flarebombs
into the air.

Even the tiny ant on the thatched roof
trembles with fear.

Always you search elsewhere
for the enemy.
But the enemy is here
and rules your universe,
reigns in you
and is everywhere.
There, in your heart,
the enemy waits
like an explosive
for its time.

High
on top
of the spiked heel
of the joy-woman's shoe,
you build your watchtower.

But the day will come
when,
singly and by millions,
the tears of our people
will meet and blend,
as trickles become ponds, streams, rivers.
The rivers will flow
and flow,
rise and rise,

until a tide of tears
flushes away
the joy-woman's lipstick and powder,
and your gold, your silver,
your power.
The flood of tears
will wash away
your garbage,
your waste,
your junk.

Written in 1966.

HERE ARE MY HANDS

Here are my hands.
Let me give them back to you,
but I pray
they will not be crushed again.

I have returned,
docile, surrendered,
without rancor at this great suffering.
I was born
under your star.
I was born for you.
I was born
to live ten thousand lives
with the heart of a child.

Here are my hands
that are also my heart, my mind,
my life—
all that remains.
Their sole power is
having bled
on the frets of love.

Here are my hands.
Let me give them back to you.
Remember,
Mother taught us to love
the withered grass on tombs

even so,
the blooming roses.

For them,
as for everything,
love is
the immaculate morning dew.

Here are my hands.
With bowed head, I give them to you.
Look, the old wounds have yet to heal.
Their blood is still fresh,
and on the fingertips,
your soul may rest
as the dew rests,
glistening
on the trembling blades of grass.

Here are my hands,
reborn once again
but still carrying old wounds.
And here is my smile
because I never hated.
And here is my heart,
my pure heart
from days gone by.

Here are my hands,
brought back to you
unhealed beneath their bandages.
I pray
they will not be crushed again.

And I beg
the stars
to be my witness.

This poem goes along with my short story, "The Naive Young Man" (not yet translated into English).

CONTEMPLATION

Since the moon is full tonight,
let us call upon the stars in prayer.
The power of concentration,
seen through the bright, one-pointed mind,
is shaking the universe.

All living beings are present tonight
to witness the ocean of fear
flooding the Earth.

Upon the sound of the midnight bell,
everyone in the ten directions joins hands
and enters the meditation on *Mahakaruna*.

Compassion springs from the heart,
as pure, refreshing water,
healing the wounds of life.

From the highest peak of the Mind Mountain,
the blessed water streams down,
penetrating rice fields and orange groves.

The poisonous snake drinks
a drop of this nectar
from the tip of a blade of grass,
and the poison on its tongue vanishes.

Mara's arrows
are transformed
into fragrant flowers.

The wondrous action of the healing water—
a mysterious transformation!
A child now holds the snake in her innocent arms.

Leaves are still green in the ancient garden.
The shimmering sunlight smiles on the snow,
and the sacred spring still flows toward the East.

On Avalokita's willow branch,
or in my heart,
the healing water is the same.

Tonight all weapons
fall at our feet
and turn to dust.

One flower,
two flowers,
millions of little flowers
appear in the green fields.

The gate of deliverance opens
with a smile on the lips
of my innocent child.

This is a metta *(love) meditation to produce the balm of* amrita *(immortality) that can transform our hearts and the world. Compassion will flow like healing waters coming from the mountaintop. When the water penetrates into the fields below, everyone benefits. The cobra, after drinking just one drop, feels the poison disappear. The little child holds the cobra without being harmed. The arrows shot by Mara become flowers.*

This poem was attacked by the communists, because they did not understand the images. They said that I was condemning them as Mara, that I was "shooting" at them, that I was advocating living with the American imperialists, the "cobra," who, they said, could never be compassionate. My poem along with this criticism was printed in a Hanoi magazine in 1965.

Even my essay "A Rose for Your Pocket" was attacked by the National Liberation Front, who said that "Thich Nhat Hanh advises people to stick to their personal mother in order to forget the motherland." I had written an article in a Saigon magazine comparing Buddhism and Marxism, saying that both begin at the same starting point—realizing the First Noble Truth—but very soon they diverge. The Buddhists experience suffering and want to make compassion the source of energy for action, but the Marxists use anger as energy.

THE FIRE THAT CONSUMES MY BROTHER

The fire that burns him
burns in my body.
And the world around me
burns with the same fire
that burns my brother.

He burns.
His figure dominates the mountain,
and the giant torch of his body fills the jungle.

O my brother,
let me kneel
upon the precious ashes
of your flesh and bones.
Let me summon your young spirit from the shadows
and give it life
in the form of a flower,
the first lotus of the season,
before anyone has picked it,
the first new bloom before the sun goes down.

I hear you now.
The storm screams with your cries.
Hearing you,
each cell in me, O my brother,
brims with tears.

I still hear you,
your appeal from heaven or hell,

and I turn to you,
wherever you are.

For a moment the world's heart stops,
while Earth looks at Sky,
and each one asks,
"Where is high and where is low?"
Your name
in the blinking stars
has been inscribed in space.

The fire that burns you
burns my flesh
with such pain,
that all my tears are not enough
to cool your sacred soul.

Deeply wounded, I remain here
keeping your hopes and promises for the young.
I will not betray you—
are you listening?
I remain here
because your very heart
is now my own.

Written in 1963 after the burning of a young monk, during the struggle against the Diêm regime. I was in New York lecturing at the Graduate School of Columbia University. I started a campaign to support the struggle of the Buddhists in Vietnam and submitted documents concerning the persecution of the Buddhists to the United Nations. As a result, the UN sent a fact-finding delegation to Vietnam.

IN MEMORY OF ALFRED HASSLER

The moment you were shown the lotus
that bloomed in the sea of fire,
you became a companion.
The torch lighted
the Committee of Conscience
carried by the *New York Times*,
bringing a message to thousands of friends.
Day and night,
efforts were made
to stop the killing.

Sitting outside the door of Thich Tri Quang,
you became the Venerable Thich Alfred Hassler.
As a friendly smile was offered,
the message of trust was transmitted.

The Menton Conference
on the beautiful French Riviera
and the retreats at the Royaumont Cloister
brought about Dai Dong.
The bell of awareness began to sound.
Five thousand scientists raised their voices
for Gaia, the Earth goddess.
One body—suddenly tens of thousands of bodies—
the path to the future was opened.
We began to have more Kloppenburgs; more De Graafs.
One flag carried the faces of children among flowers.
Who says that today De Graaf is absent?
Kloppenburg, absent?
Hassler, absent?

You are still with us as solid companions.
The march is as strong and joyful as ever,
and also our friendship.

This body is not you.
You are life without boundaries.
You have never been born, you will never die.
We have always been glad together and will always be.
We see you now and hold your hand in ours.
My body is one with the body of all species.
Alfred! Your true body is visible to us.
We see you smiling your wonderful smile.
Let us look at the magnolia flowers in Shadowcliff.

This poem was offered to Alfred Hassler and his family at Alfred's memorial service at Fellowship of Reconciliation in Nyack, New York, June 1991.

THE TORCH OF POETRY IS STILL SHINING

The torch of poetry is still shining.
Tonight, when he has reassumed his original form
in the heavenly palace,
the soul of his poetry is still
in transmigration in the midst of men.
His powerful brush, like a branch of plum blossoms,
could never be suppressed,
and the torch of his poetry will shine forever
in the history of mankind.

"To be or not to be":
the question is like the mist on the ocean,
but the path of his return is already clear on the horizon.
Whether the song is offered in an awakened or a dreamed state,
it comes from the same lute.
The fire of his courage is capable of lifting
the sorrowful curtain of the night.

Poetry soars up into the open sky like a snow-white dove.
The sound of the rising tide echoes in all directions.
As a butterfly or as a human,
he is free to enter whatever dream he likes.

As the Pacific Ocean continues to sing her powerful song,
the race of giant fish survives.

This poem was written for Vu Hoang Chuong after his death. Through his courageous and powerful poems, he contributed greatly to the nonviolent struggle against war and religious discrimination led by the Buddhists in Vietnam in the period 1963–1976.

A FREE WHITE CLOUD

I remember
when you were still a white cloud
floating freely
wherever you wanted to go.

I too was following my own course as a stream,
seeking its way to the immense ocean.

You enjoyed listening to the chanting pines
on the high peaks.
I moved up and down,
in and out,
on the white crest
of the infinite waves.

Seeing the world of humans suffer so much,
their tears becoming rivers,
you transformed yourself into rain.
Raindrop after raindrop fell each winter night.
White clouds covered the whole sky.
The sun agonized
in such darkness.

You called me back.
You called to me
to take my hands
and create a powerful storm together.

How could we not struggle
when even the prairie flowers
and mountain grass
moaned from the pain of injustice?

You lifted up your angelic arms,
determined to release the chains of oppression.

War and darkness enveloped everything.
The dark barrel of the gun—the utmost violence—
bones heaped up into mountains,
and blood flowing into rivers.

Even after your hands were crushed,
my dear, the chains were not removed.

I called the thunder back close to your side.
We were determined to confront violence.

You were brave.
During the darkness of the night,
you transformed yourself into a lion king
and let out a powerful roar.
In the foggy night,
tens of thousands of evil spirits
heard your roar
and shivered,
filled with fear.

But fearlessly,
you never stepped back,
even while so many layers of traps and dangers
were before us.
You looked calmly at the violence
as if it weren't there.

What is the nature of life and death?
How could life and death pressure us?

You called my name with a smile.

Not a single moan came from you,
even under chains and torture.

Now you are free.
The chains can no longer confine your true body.
You return to your life as a white cloud
just like before—
a white cloud
utterly free
in the immense sky.

Coming and going—
it's up to you.
When you want to have a look, you just stop.

As for me,
I am still on the crest of the waves,
singing for you
this epic song.

This poem was written for Thich Thien Minh, one of the most brilliant monks I ever knew. He served the Vietnamese Buddhists from 1949 to 1974. During the Thieu regime, many attempts on his life were made. He was sentenced to ten years of hard labor by that regime, and after the communist takeover in 1975, on October 18, 1978, he was detained in a reeducation camp. Thich Thien Minh was tortured to death in prison. I received a telegram in France three days after his death, and we spent the entire night preparing documents about him that we could release to the press in Paris the next day. I composed this poem afterwards.

EAST AND WEST

Swiftly
past the front gate
the river flows.
Like childhood memories,
clouds float.
In the backyard,
mustard flowers are ablaze
where the lost butterflies
hover.

Within his arms a firmament
beneath the warm sun,
his and mine.
Grapefruit blossoms in my hair
are no strange fragrance
for him.

My small hands, night and day,
trace the soul of the calligrapher
who rests his pen
to teach the child—
ancestral rivers and mountains
on my shoulders.
Two cultures, East and West,
bend the carrying pole down.
A rooster crows,
and over pillows the heart whispers,
"Is it dawn yet, over there?"

All winter long,
the red fire smolders
and our faith is warmed.
He sings poems,
and his voice rings clear
in the snowy sky.
To keep alive the future,
he eats meals of pickles and rice.

When spring returns to the hills,
the sky is blue as eyes are blue,
and far away flame tree blossoms burst forth.
Half a world of love
has opened halfway.

This poem was written for Hue Lien.

THE EMPTY PATH

In the shiver
of cold dew,
the lake's mirror ripples.
In the cold dawn,
your footprints leave their mark
on the untrodden grass.

Not one *lakka* leaf has fallen here.
But, after a barbaric cycle,
the warm soul of autumn has returned.
The skiff sails back to the old wharf,
carrying moonlight in its hood.

Written in 1966. I sent it as a postcard to Sister Chân Không. She received it
the day she went to prison for printing and carrying antiwar literature.

THE FRUIT OF AWARENESS IS RIPE

My youth
an unripe plum.
Your teeth have left their marks on it.
The tooth marks still vibrate.
I remember always,
remember always.

Since I learned how to love you,
the door of my soul has been left wide open
to the winds of the four directions.
Situation calls for change.
The fruit of awareness is already ripe,
and the door can never be closed again.

Fire consumes this century,
and mountains and forests bear its mark.
The wind howls across my ears,
while the whole sky shakes violently in the snowstorm.

Winter's wounds lie still,
missing the frozen blade,
restless, tossing and turning
in agony all night.

I MET YOU IN THE ORPHANAGE YARD

Your sad eyes
overflowed
with loneliness and pain.
You saw me.
You turned your face away.
Your hands drew circles
in the dusty ground.

I dared not ask you
where your father or mother was.
I dared not open up your wounds.
I only wished to sit with you a moment
and say a word or two.

O you small ones
of four or five—
your life buds already cut off,
already engulfed
by cruelty, hatred, and violence.

Why? Why?
My generation,
my cowardly age,
must shoulder the blame.

I'll go in a moment,
and you will remain
in the shabby yard.
Your eyes will return
to your familiar yard

and your fingers will draw again
those small circles
of pain
in the dusty ground.

THE DAY I GET RID OF MY HEART

My brother, the one with brown skin, is hungry. Hell is right here. I was not mindful, and you took away my part of the steak.

My brother, the one with yellow skin, is destitute. His little boy fainted in school this morning, because he lacked even a small sweet potato to eat. I was busy struggling to prevent my landlord from raising the rent. You equipped your company with new machines, and I lost my job.

My brother, the one with black skin, cannot feed his children, but his wife continues to bring forth new babies. "Oh, how could you?" He said, "What can I do?" With no milk, no rice, no potatoes, the woman left her baby along the roadside, hoping someone with a kind heart would take him home. I am so busy struggling for better wages, I am so busy night and day fighting the high cost of living, how can I find time to come and help?

My brother, the one with white skin, practices three times eight. He does not eat or sleep like the rest of his family. He is so nervous that he beats his wife and terrorizes his children. Hell is there. Our struggle is there. How can we lend a hand to a brother so far away?

You said, "In the interest of the nation, we cannot stop development." Knowing I am without a job, you offer me a position in your company making bombs and guns to sell to faraway countries. My children are hungry, my wife is crying, and I almost give in. But our brothers there need food. Why do you send them bombs and guns to kill each other?

Because I was not mindful, you took away my steak. Because I was neglectful, you took away the color TV, the Mustang, and the resort house by the sea. You tell me it is easy to have a car and a TV, I only have to sign on the dotted line and work for you. I am already bound by so many things, I do not want to enter another maze. You say I am crazy, that I am a snail who cannot carry even my own shell while I think about shouldering the Himalayan Mountains.

You used the grain that could have fed my brother to produce your steak, and your pile of steaks is now so high that it hides the sun. I cannot see the face of my beloved. The handful of grain that could have saved the starving child in Uganda was used instead to produce the liquor that you pour on the mountain of steaks while blood is being poured on our planet. How can I solve my problems if I keep thinking about my brother? The day I get rid of my heart, I assure you, that will be the day of my victory.

This was written after I met a number of people who sincerely wanted to do something for their brothers and sisters in the world, but were so busy with daily things—like eating steak or drinking wine—that they were not able to do anything even for their brothers and sisters right around them, not to mention those in developing countries.

BABITA

Her eyes open wide
as she nestles in my arms,
her whole body shivering,
her cries like tiny wails.
Babita does not dare scream aloud.
She has been brought here suddenly,
as to a holy sanctuary.
My hands also shake
as I stroke her hair
and whisper soothing words
she cannot understand.
But slowly Babita calms down,
calms down,
and rests quietly
in my arms.

My dear, I want to take into my arms
all the young orphans
two-and-a-half years old.

They have left her here to join the revolution.
Babita can wait
for months without her mother's milk,
crawling on the dirt yard,
playing in excrement,
mucus running down her face into the dirt.

Babita is still young.
Babitá can wait
for the victory of the revolution.

This was written in 1975, while I was visiting the communities of the ex-untouchable Buddhists in rural India.

THE BOAT PEOPLE

You stay up late tonight, my brothers.
This I know,
because the boat people
on the high seas
never dare to sleep.
I hear the cry of the winds
around me—
total darkness.

Yesterday they threw the dead bodies
of their babies and children
into the water.
Their tears once again filled
the ocean of suffering.
In what direction are their boats drifting
at this moment?

You stay up late tonight, brothers,
because the boat people
on the high seas
are not certain at all that humankind exists.
Their loneliness
is so immense.

The darkness has become one with the ocean;
and the ocean, an immense desert.

You stay up all night, brothers,
and the whole universe
clings to your being awake.

This poem was written in English during a conference in Singapore in 1976.

A LOTUS JUST BLOOMED ON THE OCEAN

A lotus just bloomed on the ocean.
A baby was born amidst the waves.

At midnight this January 30th,
two hundred eighty-one people aboard the Roland
pray silently,
their eyes on the ocean.
The eight-member crew directs the ship
south towards Tioman Island.
They are without water
and hope to refill the tank.

The waves tap on the sides of the boat,
punctuating the prayers.

The moon has already disappeared.
Only the light of the stars
shines the way for you to enter life, little one.
Down below, the waves are shaking their silvery heads.

The mother, lying on the bare deck,
does not have a private room
to welcome her newborn.
And the doctor,
also one of the wandering boat people,
stands up to address the others
with the good news.
The cries of the baby entering life
are swept away by the wind.
The mother smiles faintly,

and two hundred eighty-one people clap their hands
as the captain announces,
"We are heading south,
and our population is now two hundred eighty-two.
Let us give thanks to Buddha and to God."

The small radio linking the ship to shore
transmits the good news to the continent.
The human race is still there.
Tonight, on solid land, they learn of the coming into life
of Rolanda Thi Nguyen.

Where do you come from, little one,
and where are you going?
Why did you choose to come to life on this wandering boat?

She does not ask questions,
but we have to give answers.
Who has the heart to let the tiny lotus flower
that bloomed at midnight on the waves
perish in the depths of the ocean?

Brother, Sister, tell me,
where should we bring her?
We need your help.

*In 1976, during an operation to help the boat people, a baby was born on
one of the boats we hired, the* Roland. *When we received the news that she
was born, I wrote this poem.*

A PRAYER FOR LAND

Lost in the tempests
on the open seas,
our small boats drift.
We seek for land
during endless days and endless nights.

We are the foam,
floating on the vast ocean.
We are the dust,
wandering in endless space.
Our cries are lost
in the howling wind.

Without food or water,
our children lie exhausted
until they can cry no more.

We thirst for land
but are turned back from every shore.
Our distress signals rise and rise again,
but the passing ships do not stop.
How many boats have perished?
How many families lie beneath the waves?

Lord Jesus, do you hear the prayer of our flesh?
Bodhisattva Kwan Yin, do you hear our voice?
O fellow humans, do you hear our voice
from the abyss of death?
O solid shore,
we long for you!

We pray for mankind to be present today.
We pray for land to stretch its arms to us.
We pray that hope be given us today,
from this very land.

*Our intention was to carry boatloads of refugees to Australia and Guam.
We were working underground and we had prepared the* Roland *to sail to
Darwin. I wrote this poem in early 1977 and translated it into French and
English to inform journalists at the points of debarkation to cover the story
and not let the authorities push the refugees back to sea.*

LET US PRAY FOR DARKNESS
O SPARKLING STARS

The boat is gone—
great sea,
pink dawn.
I remain on the shore
counting the footprints left on the sand.
A group of anxious men and women are here
to see the boat off
and to pray for the man who is going.
"May the sea be calm and the sky quiet," they whisper.
O wind, carry their prayer
and let the ocean give him the storms they need.

O suffering,
come here by my side
and watch the boat's pilot,
who is contemplating sky and cloud,
smile calmly at waves and ocean,
not praying for the calmness of ocean and sky
but for two arms and one heart.

O suffering,
come close by my side.
Give up your haughty laugh.
Thanks to you, he will reach greatness.
Without you, he would have remained only he, forever.

Let us pray that the darkness becomes deeper,
O innumerable, twinkling stars!
At sunrise we will be able to see

sparkling streams of morning light
flowing down from the top of the mountain.

Night and day are opposite,
but night and day engender each other.

O innocent child,
are you an exiled spirit newly set down
into this worn world?
Do not look at me that way,
with your wrinkled forehead.
You are still a stranger here.
Smile in the fragrance
of this pink dawn.

Smile, young one.
Moon, cloud, and wind are all calm,
peaceful, harming nothing.
Smile, little child, as I did in early innocence,
knowing nothing, discerning nothing.
Close your ears to my words.
Remain amazed and in wonder as you are.
Return to the place you came from.

If, one day, you need me,
and I should be absent,
please listen deeply to the murmur of a spring
or the thunder of a cascade.
Contemplate the yellow chrysanthemums,
the violet bamboo,

the white cloud,
or the clear, peaceful moon.

All of them tell the same story
I tell the singing birds today.

This marvelous song you hear this morning,
little birds,
rises from uncounted suffering lives.
These lotus flowers that calmly perfume the air
reach upward from the muddy pond.
I am here, little child,
waiting for you.

This poem was written in 1956.

PLEASE CALL ME BY MY TRUE NAMES

Don't say that I will depart tomorrow—
even today I am still arriving.

Look deeply: every second I am arriving
to be a bud on a spring branch,
to be a tiny bird, with still-fragile wings,
learning to sing in my new nest,
to be a caterpillar in the heart of a flower,
to be a jewel hiding itself in a stone.

I still arrive, in order to laugh and to cry,
to fear and to hope.
The rhythm of my heart is the birth and death
of all that is alive.

I am a mayfly metamorphosing
on the surface of the river.
And I am the bird
that swoops down to swallow the mayfly.

I am a frog swimming happily
in the clear water of a pond.
And I am the grass-snake
that silently feeds itself on the frog.

I am the child in Uganda, all skin and bones,
my legs as thin as bamboo sticks.
And I am the arms merchant,
selling deadly weapons to Uganda.

I am the twelve-year-old girl,
refugee on a small boat,
who throws herself into the ocean
after being raped by a sea pirate.
And I am the pirate,
my heart not yet capable
of seeing and loving.

I am a member of the politburo,
with plenty of power in my hands.
And I am the man who has to pay
his "debt of blood" to my people
dying slowly in a forced-labor camp.

My joy is like spring, so warm
it makes flowers bloom all over the Earth.
My pain is like a river of tears,
so vast it fills the four oceans.

Please call me by my true names,
so I can hear all my cries and laughter at once,
so I can see that my joy and pain are one.

Please call me by my true names,
so I can wake up
and the door of my heart
could be left open,
the door of compassion.

*This poem was written in 1978, during the time of helping the boat people.
It was first read at a retreat in Kosmos Center in Amsterdam, Holland, orga-
nized by Niko Tideman. Daniel Berrigan was there.*

After the Vietnam War, many people wrote to us in Plum Village. We received hundreds of letters each week from the refugee camps in Singapore, Malaysia, Indonesia, Thailand, and the Philippines, hundreds each week. It was very painful to read them, but we had to be in contact. We tried our best to help, but the suffering was enormous, and sometimes we were discouraged. It is said that half the boat people fleeing Vietnam died in the ocean; only half arrived at the shores of Southeast Asia.

There are many young girls, boat people, who were raped by sea pirates. Even though the United Nations and many countries tried to help the government of Thailand prevent that kind of piracy, sea pirates continued to inflict much suffering on the refugees. One day, we received a letter telling us about a young girl on a small boat who was raped by a Thai pirate.

She was only twelve, and she jumped into the ocean and drowned herself. When you first learn of something like that, you get angry at the pirate. You naturally take the side of the girl. As you look more deeply, you will see it differently. If you take the side of the little girl, then it is easy. You only have to take a gun and shoot the pirate. But we can't do that. In my meditation, I saw that if I had been born in the village of the pirate and raised in the same conditions as he was, I would now be the pirate. There is a great likelihood that I would become a pirate. I can't condemn myself so easily. In my meditation, I saw that many babies are born along the Gulf of Siam, hundreds every day, and if we educators, social workers, politicians, and others do not do something about the situation, in twenty-five years a number of them will become sea pirates. That is certain. If you or I were born today in those fishing villages, we might become sea pirates in twenty-five years. If you take a gun and shoot the pirate, you shoot all of us, because all of us are to some extent responsible for this state of affairs.

After a long meditation, I wrote this poem. In it, there are three people: the twelve-year-old girl, the pirate, and me. Can we look at each other and recognize ourselves in each other? The title of the poem is "Please Call Me by My True Names," because I have so many names. When I hear one of these names, I have to say, "Yes."

THE FISHERMAN AND THE FISH

You are the fisherman
on the great ocean drawing your net,
your skin smelling of the fragrance of the sea,
your arm muscles fold under the great sun.

I am the fish
with shining fins and scales,
together with thousands of others
struggling desperately in your net.

I lie agonizing at the bottom of your boat.
You have caught me
because you need to live.

You are also the woman
holding her shopping basket,
looking around the marketplace.
I am already dead,
but my eyes are not yet closed.
My flesh is still fresh,
and my gills still very red.

You brought me home,
cut me into small pieces
to add to your pot.
Hot soup awaits
this evening's winter's dinner,
and you and your children,
under your sheltered roof, are satisfied.
No one asks the question

of what I have become.
Can anyone recognize my identity
when form and emptiness
are of the same reality?

Having undergone a thousand million lifetimes
as a fish swimming in a river,
or one swimming the great ocean,
I have journeyed everywhere.
My home is space, is a palace,
my world full of corals, of sea fungi,
in blues and purples and many colors,
sometimes looking like emeralds.

In shoals with millions of other fishes,
I have traveled
back and forth,
back and forth,
freely,
happily.
But throughout all these lifetimes,
I have also tried to practice.
So that every time
I got caught in your net,
I could die peacefully,
without vengeance,
without despair,
because I know
life is made of death,
being is made of nonbeing,
all is interdependent,
and you and I,
we contain each other.

BUTTERFLIES OVER THE GOLDEN MUSTARD FIELDS

For ten years
we had a beautiful green garden.
For twenty years
the sun always shone on our thatched roofs.
My mother came out and called me home.
I came to the front yard
near the kitchen
to wash my feet
and warm my hands over the rosy hearth,
waiting for our evening meal
as the curtain of night
fell slowly on our village.

I will remain a child
no matter how long I live.
Just yesterday, I saw a band
of golden butterflies fluttering above our garden.
The mustard greens were bursting with bright yellow flowers.

Mother and sister, you are always with me.
The gentle afternoon breeze is your breathing.
I am not dreaming of some distant future.
I just touch the wind and hear your sweet song.
It seems like only yesterday that you told me,
"If one day you find everything destroyed,
then look for me in the depths of your heart."

I am back. Someone is singing.
My hand touches the old gate,

and I ask, "What can I do to help?"
The wind replies,
"Smile. Life is a miracle.
Be a flower.
Happiness is not built of bricks and stones."

I understand. We don't want to cause each other pain.
I search for you day and night.
The trees grope for one another in the stormy night.
The lightning flash reassures them
they are there for one another.

My brother, be a flower standing along the wall.
Be a part of this wondrous being.
I am with you. Please stay.
Our homeland is always within us.
Just as when we were children,
we can still sing together.

This morning, I wake up and discover
that I've been using the sutras as my pillow.
I hear the excited buzzing of the diligent bees
preparing to rebuild the universe.
Dear ones, the work of rebuilding
may take thousands of lifetimes,
but it has also already been completed
just that long ago.
The wheel is turning,
carrying us along.
Hold my hand, brother, and you will see clearly

that we have been together
for thousands of lifetimes.

My mother's hair is fresh and long.
It touches her heels.
The dress my sister hangs out to dry
is still sailing in the wind
over our green yard.

It was an autumn morning
with a light breeze.
I am really standing in our backyard—
the guava trees, the fragrance of ripe mangoes,
the red maple leaves scurrying about
like little children at our feet.

A song drifts from across the river.
Bales of silky, golden hay
traverse the bamboo bridge.
Such fragrance!

As the moon rises above
the bamboo thicket,
we play together
near the front gate.

I am not dreaming.
This is a real day, a beautiful one.
Do we want to return to the past
and play hide-and-seek?

We are here today,
and we will be here tomorrow.
This is true.
Come, you are thirsty.
We can walk together
to the spring of fresh water.
Someone says that God has consented
for mankind to stand up and help Him.
We have walked hand in hand
since time immemorial.
If you have suffered, it is only
because you have forgotten
you are a leaf, a flower.

The chrysanthemum is smiling to you.
Don't dip your hands into cement and sand.
The stars never build prisons for themselves.

Let us sing with the flower and the morning birds.
Let us be fully present.
I know you are here because I can look into your eyes.
Your hands are as beautiful as chrysanthemums.
Do not let them be transformed
into gears, hooks, and ropes.

Why speak of the need to love one another?
Just be yourself.
You don't need to become anything else.

Let me add here one testimony of my own.
Please listen as if I were
a bubbling spring.

And bring mother. I want to see her.
I will sing for you, my dear sister,
and your hair will grow as long as mother's.

*This poem was begun in 1963 in New York, just before I returned to Viet-
nam. Following the fall of Diêm, my brother monks asked me to leave
Columbia University and help with the work of rebuilding the country.
When I went to Vietnam, I developed this poem more fully. It is about
rebuilding the country and about the kind of action known as "non-action."
We don't have to do much if we know how to be. If we stop being joyful and
stop singing, we are caught in a kind of prison. The stars in the sky never
build prisons.*

I AM BACK TO OPEN THE OLD PAGES

Suddenly I welcome myself back.
The reference point is no longer seen,
and last night's dream is full of illusory images.
The walls that help stop the winds and the rain
have formed a corner of warm space.
The flickering candles
evoke the incense perfume of a New Year's Eve.
It rains.
Inside the house, dinner is served.
A few leaves of coriander
bring back the forms of the homeland.
Suddenly all frontiers are removed
just because of the midday storm,
and everything is revealed.
Isn't today's sun the same as yesterday's?

Birds seen against the color of the purple evening.
The two ends of time join
and tenderly push me
into a new opening.
The curtains of the evening,
destined to catch space,
suddenly become weeping willows.
Clouds are calling each other
to meet at the mountain's summit.

I am back. I find myself opening the old pages.
The blazing sunset has burned up all certificates.
Wordy mantras have proven to be powerless.
The wind is blowing hard.

Out there at the end of the sky,
the flapping wings of some strange bird.
Where am I?
The point of concentration is remembrance.
The real home is childhood with its grassy hills.
The violet *tía tô* leaves contain an autumn that is fully ripe.
Your small feet treading the path
are like drops of dew on young leaves.
My letters sent to you
are like the church bells.
A golden sky of flowers is contained in a mustard seed.
I join my palms
and let
a flower bloom
wonderfully in my heart.

HOMELAND

My homeland is right here
with banana groves, bamboo thickets, rivers, oats.
The earth beneath is full of dust.
But every time I lift up my face,
I always see beautiful stars.

THE SONG OF NO COMING
AND NO GOING

When I left home, I was a child.
Now I return an old man.
Villagers still speak with the same accent,
but my hair and beard are completely white.
The village children see me but don't recognize me.
They look at each other and giggle,
"Where have you come from, old sir?"

Where have you come from, old sir?
"I have come from the same place you have,
yet you don't know there is a link between us."
I stroke my snow-white beard this morning.
The young leaves on the trees are new and green.
They see no link between themselves and the seed
that took root so many years ago on this very land.
Villagers still speak with the same accent,
but after so many years, the village has become your village.
To your puzzled eyes, I am only a strange, old visitor
arriving from some unknown world.
To come or to go, to depart or return—
who among us is not a wanderer?

Where have you come from, old sir?
You don't see. How could you?
Even if I sing to you the old songs I learned in this village,
I would still be a stranger in your eyes.
When I tell you, "This is my village,"
your eyes dance and you laugh.
And I laugh too, when you say I am just telling a story.

The bamboo trees, the riverbank, the village hall—
everything is still here.
They have changed, yet they haven't.
A new bamboo shoot, a new red-tiled roof,
a new small lane,
a new child—
What is the purpose of my return?
I don't know.
There is a haunting image of the past.
The traveler has no real point of departure
and no point of arrival.
Who is he, this explorer of the triple worlds?

As if to a former life—
the sweet potatoes and turnips, the hay, the cottage—
I come back to my village.
But those with whom I worked and sang
are strangers to those I find today.
Everywhere are the children,
the red-tiled roofs,
the narrow lanes—
The past and the future look at each other,
and the two shores suddenly become one.
The path of return continues the journey.

*I wrote this poem in early 1967 after visiting Heidelberg Castle. That day
I had the clear impression that I had been there before, although it was
my first visit. The poem was also inspired by a four-line poem written by
a Chinese poet of the Tang dynasty: "I left home when I was a child. Now
I return with white hair and a white beard. But the dialect of the village is
still the same. The children see me but do not recognize me. They laugh and
ask, 'Where have you come from, old sir?'" This poem is about non-coming
and non-going. The Path of Return Continues the Journey is the title of*

a play I wrote to pay homage to Nhat Chi Mai, who burned herself to death calling for peace and reconciliation in Vietnam, and for the four School of Youth for Social Service workers who were killed in mission.

One of the titles of the Buddha is Tathagata, *the one who has come from suchness (ultimate reality), and who will go to suchness. There is an explanation of this term in the* Diamond Sutra *that a Tathagata means one who has come from nowhere and will go nowhere. The "Triple World" is the world of desire, that of form, and that of non-form. When a person is liberated from the three worlds, he or she can be called emancipated.*

Life and death, past and future are often thought of as opposing each other and not to be found in one reality. That is not true. "The two shores suddenly become one." I was thinking of the two shores separated by what we call death. When a man dies, he is separated from his beloved one by something like a river that he cannot cross. But is it really so? There is a river separating the two shores, but you can always use a boat. "The past and the future look at each other." And when they look at each other, their eyes mirror one another.

In my tradition, people say that if you respect an old man, you will live a long life. If you don't, you will die young. In the Vietnamese home, we usually see three generations living together, sometimes four. Old people take care of the grandchildren. It is the grandparents who tell fairy tales to their grandchildren. They need each other. The old people have become children again. It's very natural they play together. The young couple thinks more of the future. Sometimes they consider their old parents as young children. They love them as children. All these elements may be useful for understanding this poem.

EXISTENCE

It is night.
Rain pelts the roof.
The soul awakens
to a flooded Earth—
a sea of storm
roaring,
then passing.

In that short moment,
shifting lines and shapes,
fleeting,
barely seen.

Before the passing moment tilts
and falls to melancholy,
laughter sounds
in quiet raindrops.

This poem was written in Saigon in 1965. It was raining hard. There was so much death and killing, so much destruction. And yet in one moment, I could hear the laughter in a raindrop.

LITTLE STAR

Where have you been, little star?
I have been looking for you everywhere
out of my window among the dark clouds.
Where have you been?
I feel so forlorn,
like a small bird lost on a foggy island.

It has been raining for nights.
The town is so chilly and deserted.
Late at night on the sidewalk
I see the silhouettes of lonely, wet forms.

Resting my head on a stack of books
like the ancient poets,
I have tried to call up your image
from deep in my consciousness,
while the rain and the wind continue to rage.

Tonight as I bend over my desk,
my head held in my two hands,
I cannot imagine that the wind
has carried away all the clouds.
The sky is clear.
The rain has stopped longing for your call.
I am surprised to see you are there
through the window.
You have returned.

Dear little star,
you have been through such storms, rain, and wind.

Where did you go?
For how long and on what strange land
have you been weeping?
You have come back.
Your eyes are still lost in surprise
as you watch me through the window.
Where have you been on these stormy days?
Your little body, battered by countless winds,
still shivers with cold.
Resting peacefully at the bottom of the crystal cup,
with tears in your eyes, you recall:
"Today the Kingdom of Heaven held
a great festival for thousands of stars.
The sky is clear.
The clouds have all blown away.
I went up to that kingdom
and knelt down for our homeland and prayed
that the anguish, the killing,
the disasters of flood, fire, and cruelty
in our poor land would end."

Your voice has reached millions of stars
that all transformed into wonderful teardrops
trembling in the air.
I am sending deep thanks to ten thousand little stars
whose faith is diamond-strong.
You are like flowers blooming,
shining brilliantly in the vast realm of consciousness.
My little star, you are back home.
With tears in my eyes,
I call your name
and feel the warmth in my heart.

ULTIMATE
DIMENSION

THE SOUND OF A GREAT BIRD

The old path
and his footprints—
the perfume of time does not smell of the violet;
the color of time is not the color of the sky.

Dust on my way,
moss on the wild stone,
soot on the old wood—
time is not flowing.
The unlimited is concentrated—
above my head, the thundering sound of passing wings.

In his very hand is found
the power to open or to close.
Let the wanderer return to his starting point.
I find myself today all alone
at this crossroads
that offers both opening and closing,
mounting and descending.

In a startling moment
the echo of the ages,
the sound of the walking steps,
projected to the present
shakes me
awake.

"One open, one closed—that is Tao," is a sentence from the Tao Te Ching.
This poem was written at the same time as "Beckoning."

THE BEAUTY OF SPRING BLOCKS MY WAY

Spring comes slowly and quietly
to allow winter to withdraw
slowly and quietly.
The color of the mountain this afternoon
is tinged with nostalgia.
The terrible war flower
has left her footprints—
countless petals of separation and death
in white and violet.
Very tenderly, the wound opens itself in the depths of my heart.
Its color is the color of blood,
its nature the nature of separation.

The beauty of spring blocks my way.
How could I find another path up the mountain?

I suffer so. My soul is frozen.
My heart vibrates like the fragile string of a lute
left out in a stormy night.
Yes, it is there. Spring has really come.
But the mourning is heard
clearly, unmistakably,
in the wonderful sounds of the birds.
The morning mist is already born.
The breeze of spring in its song
expresses both my love and my despair.
The cosmos is so indifferent. Why?
To the harbor, I came alone,
and now I leave alone.

There are so many paths leading to the homeland.
They all talk to me in silence. I invoke the Absolute.
Spring has come
to every corner of the ten directions.
Its song, alas, is only the song
of departure.

1951. This was written less than twelve hours after I fell in love with a nun. It happened at the Vien Giac Temple on New Year's Eve in the beautiful village of Cau Dat in the highlands. She was twenty. Both of us realized that we wanted to continue being a monk and a nun. So we decided to depart from each other. This was not easy. I was lucky to have a loving and understanding Sangha with me at that time that made it possible. Forty-one years later, I told this love story in a twenty-one day retreat at Plum Village in English, on the theme of Vipassana meditation in the Mahayana tradition.

UNCLASP

Deserted beach,
footsteps in the sand
erased by rain—
this anguish comes from nowhere,
and its feet do not yet touch the Earth.

Suddenly I hear a far-off whisper
of the gentle winds of spring,
and the anguish is gone.

1966. A feeling of anxiety can be transformed with a few conscious breaths. The anxiety is like a cloud trying to land on me. I breathe in and out, and it vanishes.

SILENCE

The paper smells wonderful
as I turn the pages of this ancient book.
The water in my glass
smiles to me with crystal eyes.
Suddenly oceanic waves come up one after another
with their foamy heads.
A cold stone
summons the fog
up on the distant mountain
where the wind is howling hard.

I wake up.
The tip of my tongue is frozen
by the dewdrops
that have been sent to me
by a blade of grass on a late night.
Light flashes across
like the blade of a sword.
Perhaps it is the beginning of a storm.
Clouds rise very quickly.
From the East, urgently,
the sound of the horns is calling.

Where is my palm-leaf raincoat of years ago?
The winds are chasing after the leaves.
The lines and strokes
your brush used to trace
are brown,
the color of your arm,
the sweat that penetrates the rice field.

In this moment, our planet is lost
somewhere in the unknown,
and the giant bird
is shaking its wings in outer space.
Space in puddles
is splashing.
Space is exploding.
There is a sun
struggling up and down
in the ocean
like a giant fish with enormous red eyes.
My telephoto lens
is trying to catch the images of prehistory.
Look! The door is just unlocked,
and the future is let free.
For many lives,
that door has prevented the future from fleeing.

This morning on my way to the woods,
through the singing of the bird,
I know you are there, free,
free on a green path.
There are buds, flowers, and tiny leaves
waving to space.
The hand,
the hand that holds the baton of the talented artist
conducts the world of sound.
All sounds return
to this one point
of great silence,
this point
of great emptiness.

There is too much light—
too much light for a baby just entering life.
I see now
our grandmother
with her hair tied behind her head
in the form of an onion.
She is sweeping bamboo leaves.
She begins to gather the leaves into a pile
and burn them.
The smoke is rising,
warming up the sky.
The Buddha smiles behind a thin cloud.
Tonight the moon is full.

APRIL

April is back,
among trees that stand
like pillars in a cathedral.
Compassion is like the rain
that comes from mountains and forest.
The motherly hands, so wondrous,
prepared for our arrival
in the warmth and light of spring.
On the first day I was brought to life,
strange birds came from all directions to sing.
I was like a naive deer.
I looked at the blue sky,
the clear water, the young leaves.
I learned to touch
when everything from the deep Earth
was ready to spring up.

The forest is trying to put on a new dress.
The little deer looks at his image in the water.
He listens to the murmur of foreign winds
as the sap of life is rising up.
He hears the singing in every bud of life.
My homeland is the rainforest,
where there are so many ancient trees
always straining to grow higher.

Every time the light streams down onto the trees,
the perfume of the jungle floats in the sky.
Above, white clouds hover and try to protect.
There is the forest.

There is also the meadow.
And there is a stream of water to refresh the Earth.

As soon as Earth and Sky brought me to life,
I was offered music by the birds
and fragrance by the trees.

I grow up.
Music is now played by the waters of the spring.
It is the second day.
And the deer comes up close to the stream.
He tries hard to listen.
The sap runs strong, urging the flower buds
who feel too shy to bloom.
In fact, it is already the third day.
The flowers are about to bloom.
The sunshine brings joy onto the delicate petals.
The fourth day has come. The cherry blossom starts the
    festival.
Do you hear something strange in the song of April?
On the fifth day, dawn comes with a surprise.
The forest wakes up in fragrance.
All of a sudden, you appear in the heart of the rainforest.
Step by step, you walk as if you are afraid to disturb us.
The deer looks at you with surprised eyes.
At that miraculous moment, you transform yourself
into a tiny flower
clinging to Mother Earth.

The sun is up.
One of your tiny petals carries a dewdrop
imitating the sun, shining forth.

The forest doesn't seem to know that you are there,
although you have already begun to sing that immortal song.
Your song sounds as if it has been there forever
in the solemn atmosphere of the deep forest.
The little deer is still trying to find what has been born,
but it doesn't seem that something has been added,
that something is new.
It doesn't seem that you have gotten lost in the deep jungle,
because your song gets along wonderfully and harmoniously
with the concert of a season called spring.
That tiny flower seems to have been
with Mother Earth from the beginning.
The little bird turns its head to the left and right, to look at you,
letting forth a string of crystal clear jewels.
Everything is participating in the concert—
birds, flowers, trees, creeks.
No one stops to ask the question,
"How long have you been present among us?"
Your presence, O little flower in the deep rainforest!
You are part of this interbeing
that knows no beginning and no end.
You have not been born. You are just now manifested.
The jungle has finished putting on her new dress.

On the tenth day, two children appear.
We don't know where they come from.
They run through the meadow and talk to each other like birds.
Then they stop at the entrance of the forest.
The sunshine is playing something like a violin.
"April has come," the older boy murmurs
into the ear of the younger one,
as if he had just discovered something very important.

They hold hands and try to listen.
Yes, it is the eternal song of spring.
They look at each other.
"April has come to the forest."
This time, it is the younger boy
who whispers into the ear of the older.

The sunshine is so warm.
Suddenly the little deer appears at the entrance of the forest,
his feet touched with the fragrance
offered by the innumerable flowers in the heart of the jungle.
A band of butterflies, attracted by this,
approaches the little deer.
The sunshine continues to play the violin.
The creeks continue to penetrate softly into the meadow,
but the deer and the children have disappeared.
They are lost in the deep forest,
trying to find out the center of the music.

Suddenly there are terrible explosions.
A flock of iron birds has come.
Fires are spit on the meadow, creeks, and jungles.
Clouds disperse. Music is blown away.
The singing stops in all the trees.
Flowers fold up their petals. Perfumes are withdrawn.
The water stops reflecting the sky. Birds keep silent as if at night.

Finally, the iron birds are gone.
Peace is restored among the trees.
The forest is able to smile again,
and the concert resumes.
It does not seem to have been disrupted.

The good news is transmitted from leaf to leaf.
All voices are sweet.
The little deer and the children have discovered
the tiny violet flower.
(The flower has never stopped singing.)

The younger child takes the head of the deer in his arms
while the older caresses him.
Everything and everyone join in the everlasting song
of the ineffable presence.
Out there, the sunshine plays its violin.
April is whole in the forest.
Tiny streams of water penetrate
silently into the Earth,
and innumerable flowers appear
over the green meadow.

THE LITTLE BUFFALO IN PURSUIT
OF THE SUN

Somewhere among the Clouds

This time, the young novice truly did not know where his master had gone. He was certain of one thing: Early this morning, his master had gone far up the mountain to gather medicinal plants. Or maybe he was gathering a few strips of clouds hanging from the top of young pine saplings.

"Novice, why don't you invite your visitor inside your hut and offer him a nice cup of hot tea?"

"Illustrious visitor, my master left for the mountain to gather some medicinal herbs. Perhaps he will soon return . . ."

"While waiting for your master to return, invite your visitor to have a cup of tea. Why have you left him at your door for such a long time? There is so much mist that his robe is already completely wet. Can't you see it?"

"Sir, if this is urgent, let me go up the mountain to look for him. The clouds are thick, but if I cup my hands around my mouth, I can call to him: 'Master, where are you? I'm looking for you. A visitor is waiting for you.'"

"Well, novice, don't worry. If you allow me, I'll make myself at home. I simply wish to sit here, drink a cup of tea, contemplate the mountain and the forest enveloped by mist. Don't disturb your master. Let him return when he wishes. Waiting doesn't bother me."

Two giant pines marked the entrance to the path leading to the hut. The visitor was deep in thought: "Is this Cuu Lung Mountain of the Four Valleys? I told myself this morning that I wouldn't climb all the way up to this hut to see the master, but start searching for myself instead. I am a stubborn child who has wandered for thousands of lives in the cycle of birth and death. Now, I wish to go back to my parents. Full of anger and self-pity, my heart has wept for so many lifetimes. This morning, dear novice, your eyes seem to give my heart some respite. I was hesitant, but your soft and courageous eyes have filled me with light."

The visitor prostrated; his forehead touched the floor of the main sanctuary where the stone was cool.

"Here I am," he said, "I have returned. I am no longer the prodigal son. I no longer want to cling to this world of struggles and hatred. Today, I am reborn. This is the day of my rebirth. The multitude of flowers and leaves are my witnesses. I have returned. I am profoundly grateful to you, for the infinite blessing of your love. There are many clouds here, but it is in this very place that I shall see your face and my own face."

The hut hangs from the side of the mountain; behind it are many little paths. High up, nestled in the clouds, the peak has towered over the mountain since the beginning of time, guarding and protecting. Every afternoon, clouds come to crown the mountain top and wrap themselves warmly around its base. The hut sleeps in the heart of the clouds.

When the Flowers and Leaves Listen Attentively

Where is Phuong Boi, the Monastery of Fragrant Palm Leaves? Right here. Phuong Boi is a forest surrounded by tea plantations, which perfume the air from early morning. Five people are walking to the foot of the hill in order to taste a young tea plant, bitter and fragrant, sharp and refreshing. The little path is welcoming. On either side, the leaves listen attentively. Each leaf, each flower, is an ear. Crimson foxgloves stand tall to listen and understand. Each leaf is also a hand outstretched. What are you listening to so attentively? To these passersby who speak like poets? They express deep feelings that have remained unchanged for thousands of lifetimes.

The breeze that caresses the hill, the fresh grass of April, the murmur of the stream in summer, the halo of clouds around the mountain top, the twittering of birds, the song of the reeds, have they all shared the same language? The green reed and yellow flower are reflections of the soul. The moon half hidden in the white clouds is also a wonderful manifestation.

Dear friends, pay attention, listen. These passersby talk to themselves, just as you do, standing between earth and sky, in this sublime reality. Let us be their witness. There are five or six or nine people walking together. Sometimes, there is only one. They have passed by here, caressing us with their hands. Their eyes shone with a thousand sparks when they noticed our presence. We are not illusions in a dream: lavender, green; straight lines, curved lines; paths, near and far; masses of stars of five different colors; small bouquets of rosy sunshine; the long, pale pink fingers.

We have welcomed, greeted, and accepted them in our midst. We remain peacefully in the palms of their hands, that have cherished us and lavished so much attention and care on us. My dear older sister eucalyptus, stretch out your long branches loaded with leaves right to their tips. My dear little sister lily, young bud, smile! Life is full. Nothing is wasted, nothing is superfluous in the kingdom this morning. Our dear sun is still here. This afternoon, perhaps I will depart; tomorrow, my children will bloom. The flowers and leaves of tomorrow will forever be present, therefore I will always be present. Let us support them together. They have made the great vow. No sooner do I receive the message than I transmit it. It will pass from leaf to leaf, from branch to branch.

The Clouds on the Mountain Top

The message reached the mountain top, and the white clouds heard it. The branches and leaves high up on the mountain waved their hands. The great vow inscribed on a page of the great book of life changed into a script of moon and stars and unfurled into a magnificent cloud. Droplets of water flew up high. Who has the power to capture a net of dew pearls?

Tomorrow, the clouds will thicken and fall down as rain. The message will penetrate the five continents and the four oceans. This morning, it will touch its native land of Phuong Boi, the Monastery of Fragrant Palm Leaves, in the Dai Lao forest, the forest of the great age, and the little children playing in the tender green meadow; it will touch the Medford forest in a summer shower; the hermit's well on Mount Na; the rock on Mount Yen Tu, where the great master of the Bamboo Forest still dwells; it will be everywhere.

A Twilight of Perfect Clarity

Is this twilight the only thing in existence of such awesome beauty? Here are the mist, the clouds, the rivers, the water, the maple at the river's edge, the flickering light of an oil lamp on a fishing boat, yet I do not feel homesick for my country.

Lying down in the heart of my homeland, I watch the mountain through the clouds and the clouds through the mountain. Stretched out on the side of the hill, my gaze turns toward the West, through the lines of trees in the distance. The twilight is perfectly clear. Just like me, the sky and the earth are transforming in every instant. Each fraction of time is splendid, each fraction of time is sublime. I stretch out; my back rests against the soft pillow of the hill. I doze off. Life is singing, in this great reality, in each of her wonderful aspects.

One thing embraces all things. The peak guards the peace of my slumber.

The clouds rendezvous on the mountain.
They are multiplying.
The past and future no longer exist.
The present expresses itself in its fullness.
I sit down again.
The sound of the hunting horn no longer oppresses us.
The scent of the grass is intoxicating.

Laurel Leaves

Do you remember, young novice? That morning, at the foot of the hill, I showed you a sturdy laurel, and you doubted that it was indeed a laurel. How did it manage to become so big? I pinched a little leaf and squeezed it between my fingers so you could smell its fragrance. Then you confirmed that it was indeed a laurel.

I told you how I love the flavor of laurel leaves, of thyme, coriander, mint, parsley, and other aromatic herbs found in abundance in our homeland. The leaves of the river-tea-tree and the guava tree have a unique taste and fragrance, which I like so much. Although tiny, the leaf of the guava tree is the immutable emissary of a particular and incomparable scent.

Dear novice, if, in the future, we are able to journey to far-away planets, the aroma of a single laurel leaf will remind us of how much we miss our own planet, our country, and our homeland.

How marvelous is the reality of the present moment! Each leaf is a universe of taste, scent, and memories. Each one is a unique world, both spiritual and temporal. A single leaf encompasses the entire universe. We tremble at this revelation that inspires great devotion. We bow in front of the miracle of this manifestation. We no longer dare neglect the smallest thing: leaf, stone, or fragrance.

Dearest friend, your voice is yours, unique. I remember in the past I used to listen to it on a tiny cassette tape; yet it opened up a vast and bright world for me, which was its very own, a realm of past, present, and future. One day, someone told me that you had telephoned, announcing that you would come and meet me at the foot of the mountain. How strange the telephone is, this invention of ours that aims to prolong the presence of the phenomenal world.

Certain wondrous phenomena respond to the human need to know the infinite, truth, beauty, goodness. Others, deliberately enigmatic, remain inaccessible to our brains and hearts. Humans are much too accustomed to penetrating the universe with a narrow and limited mind, ignoring the eighty-thousand doors that are always open, at our disposal.

That morning, dear novice, you watched me with sparkling eyes. Now I see your eyes again, wide open like a window, that offered me a vision of the splendor of the world, of reality as it is. My child, you are the key. You are the mouthpiece of the whole universe, of ultimate reality as it manifests in yellow flowers and violet bamboo. Looking at you, I see each stone, each leaf, the entire universe. I see my true home in a young laurel bud.

Duong Xuan Hill

The osmanthus is one of the most precious flowers of Duong Xuan (springtime of Yang) Hill. The hill is mostly covered with rocks and stones. Our mother pagoda, the first pagoda built by the founding father of our lineage, was built there more than 150 years ago. The osmanthus there are scrawny; their trunks and branches are covered with whitish mold. Their fragrant white flowers cluster in little bunches, pressed between thin, angular, delicate branches.

At that time, I was as old as you, and every afternoon around three o'clock, I would pick two or three bouquets for Grandfather Monk Su-Ong's tea, for that is how we respectfully called the highest monk in our order. Few flowers bloomed at the same time, but they bloomed every season. The flowers that stayed on the branches dried up, turned yellow, and fell.

Sometimes, deep inside the tiny corollas, dark yellow insects hid. They were as tiny as grains of sand. I, the novice Phung Xuan, tried to dislodge them by shaking the flowers over a sheet of white paper. Phung Xuan is my Dharma name, connecting me to my lineage. It means "Walk towards spring." I would then lay the little bouquets on the palm of my left hand and lift them to my nostrils to inhale their perfume. How delicious! Finally, I would put them inside the teapot with a few leaves of green tea and pour the boiling water over them.

Around twelve, venerable Grandfather Monk liked his tea to be brought to his table. He would drink a few drops, just enough to wet his tongue, then pour another small cup, which he gave to the novice respectfully standing back. The novice waited to serve the tea and drink with him. What joy for a student.

The afternoons were very peaceful in our mother pagoda. The shade of the great Dharma hall unfurled its freshness on the long row of water jars lined up beside the building that sheltered Grandfather Monk Su-Ong's room. The main entrance to the Lac Nghia (Joys of Friendship) room was always open. In the center of the courtyard, the carambola tree spread out the shade of its foliage on the pond and rocks. From time to time, a yellow leaf would fall and gently lie on the surface of the water.

The ageless rocks were encrusted with moss. Big, heavy fruit hung from the tree. Everyone proclaimed that these carambolas were as sweet, if not sweeter, than the oranges from Kwang Chou. In fact, a carambola is a carambola, and an orange from Kwang Chou is an orange from Kwang Chou. Each one contains a wondrous universe. These carambolas are prized for their crunchiness. Their flesh, neither too soft nor too juicy, allows us to eat and savor them without staining our hands or clothes. Their sweet taste is unique and does not resemble an orange in the least. It is the sweet taste belonging only to the carambola. Doesn't my dear friend, Phung Xuan the novice, make you smile?

At the Tu Quang (Light of Kindness) pagoda, there was a monk named Trong An (Deep Gratitude). He had a wonderful character, very friendly and kind. He was a poet. Several monks and nuns had learned his poems by heart. His pseudonym, Truc Diep, meant Bamboo Leaf. Each year, on New Year's Day, he would go to the mother pagoda to see Grandfather Monk Su-Ong and his novice Phung Xuan. In honor of the occasion, the venerable Grandfather Monk would offer him a carambola, placed on a white plate, with a little knife for peeling it and removing the two ends. One pulls off the quarters with one's fingers and savors them. One never uses a knife to cut a star-shaped slice. Before the visitor took his leave, Phung Xuan often offered a second carambola adorned with a few leaves to decorate Trong An's room at the Tu Quang pagoda.

One does not eat a carambola while drinking tea.

The Jambosa Tree
Towards three in the afternoon, the sun's rays were still burning hot. In spite of the heat, mindful work had already resumed in

the meditation hall, in the cassava field, in the meadow, on the cliff, and in the library. His head covered by a large conical hat made of palm leaves, Grandfather Monk Su-Ong went down to the lake or up towards the pine-covered hill. He came to oversee the work, make suggestions, and everyone appreciated his refreshing presence. He always carried his bamboo stick. He would stop here and there, radiant with joy, for ten or fifteen minutes. Sometimes the novice Phung Xuan would accompany him on his visit to the bamboo groves. The young *can-giao* bamboo shoots taste good and strong.

The taste and smell of tea influenced the whole afternoon in the monastery. The novice would cut a few bamboo shoots that grew too thickly close to the ground. His arms loaded, he would bring them to Auntie Tu, who prepared them with soy sauce for dinner. On some mornings, especially after a rainy night, the novice went hunting for mushrooms with Grandfather Monk Su-Ong.

My dear children, when you return to the mother pagoda, I promise I'll take you everywhere: to the hill, to the garden, along all the paths, to the bamboo grove, to the well. Then you will learn to see with the eyes of Su-Ong, your Grandfather Monk, and with mine, that is to say, with your own eyes.

All the nooks and crannies overflow with memories. The whitewashed wall next to the Tang Thap stupa is where, many years ago, the novices Tam Man (Fullness of the Heart) and Phung Xuan used to roast can-giao bamboos and fresh mushrooms on a fire made of pine needles. The meal started with the bamboo shoots, cooked to perfection and placed on a fig leaf; their bright yellow flesh was tender and sweet-smelling. The novices enjoyed them. The meal ended with the mushrooms: morels, boletus mushrooms, chanterelles, blue-feet mushrooms, and others ... Carefully washed in the river, they were then rubbed with salt, then washed again. Finally, they were wrapped in fig leaves and laid on the fire. The novices relished them. The mushrooms were flavored with bay leaves, thyme, parsley, and mint picked in the pagoda garden.

When we are adolescents, we have a great thirst, a thirst for intimacy, for the forbidden, for fun, for mischief, a thirst to act wild. When we remember those times, we miss the bonds of friendship that we made at that age.

My children, I will bring you with me to visit the jambosa tree in the willow garden north of the pagoda. This tree has a close connection with Tam Man. His eyes were as bright as yours today. The two novices used to play under this tree for hours. Tam Man often climbed up the tree and Phung Xuan stayed down below. Tam Man threw ripe jambosas down to Phung Xuan. The two brothers played like this in the willow garden, on scorching afternoons, while other members of the community rested in their rooms.

Tam Man was younger than Phung Xuan. When you arrive at the pagoda, you will naturally become Tam Man and Phung Xuan. Nothing will have passed, nothing will be lost.

Wind

The well was made of stone and its water was icy. It was so pleasant to shower with the cool water in the evening, under a bright moon, or on summer afternoons. Two arms'-lengths of rope were all it took for the bucket to reach the water.

In the summer, Phung Xuan washed himself with the water at least once a day, sometimes two or three times. The water from the well was so refreshing. It was reserved for washing, watering plants, and washing clothes. A hedge of privets surrounded the well. The pagoda was so quiet that you could hear the sound of the bucket and the water streaming on the edge of the well from more than ten yards away. If someone was already at the well, you had to wait until he or she left before going over yourself. Tam Man and Phung Xuan didn't obey that rule. Tam Man would exclaim: "Let me come in and have my shower as well. We'll have fun."

Near the well, there was a stone basin to wash clothes in. It had a hole, as round and small as a toe, which could be stopped with a cork. It's probably no longer used today, but it is still there. You can see Phung Xuan doing his wash there. Novices drew water only from the upper well for drinking, cooking, and making tea. It was situated high up and had a cover. A small jar with a wooden top and a little scoop was placed near the tea kitchen on the path leading to the Ancestors' hall. Every morning, Phung Xuan went to the kitchen to start the fire to boil water and prepare tea for Su-Ong and the monks. In winter, our limbs froze while we made the fire. Phung Xuan wished the fire would catch quickly so he could warm up his numbed hands. You could always find small bundles of pine sticks in the kitchen that Auntie Tu had bought at An Cuu market. We used these to light the fire quickly. The kitchen was tiny and was reserved for preparing the morning tea. Nothing else could be done there.

When you return, my child, I will take you to visit Auntie Tu's tomb, the Dieu Nghiem pagoda, the Tang Thap and Lang Vien stupa, and the pagoda's mausoleums. I remember one day, in Lang Vien, when I was working as a guide for a group of students from Huê University, a wind blew up suddenly and quickly gained strength. It was very cold, and I invited the students to seek shelter inside the mausoleum. There, we were protected from the wind, which was howling among the pines. Then, a terrifying sound filled the earth and sky. A real storm! We all longed to be somewhere out of the wind. Later, I led the whole group to the kitchen where we warmed up. We stayed in its warmth for a long time.

The Trai Bui Olives and the Almond Tree

For your first meal, the novices will probably offer you some trai bui olives, a variety of smooth, purple olives that are only found in tropical countries, which are marinated in soy sauce. You can peel off their flesh with your fingers, tear it into little pieces, and dip it in a bowl of soy sauce. A novice will probably have cooked some olives with a little salted and fermented soy. You will develop such an appetite that you will want to devour all the rice in the pagoda. There are many olive trees of this variety at our mother pagoda. Each year, at harvest time, the novices offer olives to the other pagodas in the area. The pagodas Tay Thiên, Thuyen Ton, Tu Dam, Bao Quoc, Linh Mu, and Tuong Van each receive a gift of three to five hundred olives. Sometimes a pagoda that has not received its gift sends a reminder. One day, the novice Phu met a monk from Truc Lam pagoda on a mountain lane. He could not help asking him, "Have you picked many olives this year? You haven't visited us yet. It would be nice if you brought us some." The trai bui olives are truly precious.

At that time, Phung Xuan often asked himself why the other pagodas hadn't planted olive trees. Perhaps it took many decades for an olive tree to bear fruit. Our mother pagoda had about ten olive trees. The most fruitful tree was behind the West hall and the Ancestors' hall. Its trunk was very straight, and it had beautiful foliage. There was also one near the Venerable Patriarch's stupa, not far from the century-old magnolia tree. The one that grew near the stable, close to the nut tree, was also very tall.

I haven't yet told you the story of this nut tree. During the war, sometimes we had no oil in the pagoda. The novices had to gather nuts from the tree. They broke the shells and crushed the pulp so they could make dishes requiring oil. The nuts are tasty when roasted and crushed, but if you eat too many, you get a stomachache.

Chu Chi Chu Chi, Little Abbot Chu Tri

In 1964, the novice Nhat Tri (Unique Wisdom), your older brother, was accompanying me on an expedition up the river Thu Bon to help the victims of the floods. At that time, the war was raging, making our mission dangerous. The two warring factions were present in the region. Your older sister, Chân Không (True Emptiness), also accompanied us on our journey. All the members of the group were dressed in thin brown robes and walked barefoot. They were walking in full awareness, on the hard soil of Ca Tang, Son Khuong, Khuong Binh, Son Thuan, and Tu Phu regions. On either side of the river, bullets whistled by. At one point, Nhat Tri jumped in the water. When your brother wrote letters, his handwriting strangely resembled mine. You would not be able to distinguish it from mine. He was very active in starting Pilot villages, which gave birth to Tu Nguyen village (Volunteers of the Great Vow), as well as in the movement of Youth for Social Service, from 1964 to 1974.

"I am going to the field and I see a buffalo . . ." These are the first words of a song that he composed for the children of Thao Dien village. He taught at the School of Nightingales in Cau Kinh village and helped create Thao DiDien village. The children gave him the nickname "chu tri tru tri" ("the little priest Tri"), which became "chu chi chu chi" because they lisped. Your older brother was an exemplary social worker. He put all his heart into serving others. One day in a street in the capital, an American soldier spat on his head from the height of a military truck. That soldier, under the sway of propaganda, saw communists disguised as Buddhist monks everywhere. When your brother came home that evening, he cried. I held him in my arms for a long time. During a mission to help the people, he disappeared. His friends and I waited for him for fifteen years. Alas, he never came back. My child, call him by his name, for he is your older brother.

Sister Chân Không often came to our mother pagoda to see Su-Ong, the venerable grandfather. She stayed there when she came to teach at the Faculty of Sciences in Huê. The novices were happy to offer her trai bui olives and cheese made from tofu. Grandfather Monk Su-Ong also enjoyed her visits very much. She would often bring him a package of dates, a loaf of gluten ham, and a pot of honey. Once, she brought a microscope for the little novices. They all pressed their heads together to look inside. Hearing them talking and laughing out loud, Grandfather Monk Su-Ong could not resist sitting next to them and looking inside the eyepiece. When he discovered a corn pistil as big as a rope, he burst out laughing like a young novice. Young and old had the same spark in their eyes. What a wondrous scene! How can the gap between such distant generations be as thin as a hair or a thread of silk?

When you arrive at the mother pagoda, you will see Grandfather Monk Su-Ong, with his wide conical hat, coming and going along the path that leads to the pond shaped like a half-moon. Every time I returned from a long trip, he would open his eyes wide and look at me for a long time, to make sure of what he saw in front of him, before expressing his joy; a very pure joy, childlike and innocent. I feel so much gratitude for Sister Chân Không, who took care of him in my absence, during all those years of trips and difficult missions.

The Little Buffalo

During the late afternoon, while weeding, Phung Xuan could hear Tam Man chanting inside the great Dharma hall, his voice as clear and full as a bell.

When evening came, sitting at the edge of the pond, he would listen to the chanting attentively till night fell. He did not even move to go down to the half-moon pond to wash his hands. The atmosphere was strange, enchanting, and the moon was so brilliant over Duong Xuan Hill.

Everything had converged to make Phung Xuan a poet. But poetry is not just moonlight. Like me, you know that poetry is also the swampy stagnant water, outer-space fire storms, broken-down huts on the river's edge, rescue attempts, bold and dangerous acts, yellow flowers, violet bamboo, and ultimate reality, as it is.

His voice, as clear and deep as a bell, is imprinted in me forever. I live with it, in it. It lives in me. Tam Man is an adult now, and Phung Xuan, also. Nevertheless, my children, in the ultimate reality, you can meet each other as young novices in the mother pagoda. At that time, no one owned a tape recorder to record Tam Man's wonderful voice. Yet his voice is not lost. It still exists, he still exists. Phung Xuan still exists, just because you are there.

Do you see, my friend? The three of us together, Tam Man, you, our friend, and me, Phung Xuan, are running after each other at full speed on the side of the hill. Tender grass and April pines grow all around us. In the distance, we glimpse the forest.

The little river is snaking around the foot of the hill. Barefoot, with no sandals or shoes, we run as fast as we can. Look, there is a little buffalo; he has seen the three children. He also starts to run. He follows us towards the sun. Towards the sun . . .

Against the flaming sunset is the silhouette of three children . . .

TRUE SOURCE

Where will I find the Himalayan range?
In me there is a strong and graceful mountain peak,
stretching up, lost in mist and clouds.
Let us go together to climb that nameless mountain,
let us sit on the ageless blue-green stone,
quietly watching time weave the silken thread
that creates the dimension called space.

Where does the Amazon River flow?
In me a winding river makes its way.
I don't know from the depths of which mountain
it pours out.
Night and day, its silvery water
winds toward no fixed destination.
Let us go together, putting a boat
on its fiercely flowing stream,
to find our way together
to the common goal of all beings in the cosmos.

Which galaxy shall I call Andromeda?
In me there is a river of stars moving silently
with millions of brilliant stars.
Let us fly up together, tearing the net of space,
opening a way on the path of the clouds.
The sound of your flapping wings will reach
even the most distant planet.

Which species shall I call Homo sapiens?
In me there is a little boy.
His left hand lifts up the curtain of night.

His right hand holds a sunflower, his torch.
The child's two eyes are stars.
The child's hair flies curling in the wind,
like clouds over the ancient jungle on a stormy afternoon.
Let us approach the child together and ask,
"What are you looking for? Where are you going?
Where is the true source? Where is the final destination?
And what are the ways home?"

The little boy just smiles.
The flower in his hand suddenly
becomes a bright red sun,
and the child goes on alone—
his path through the stars.

I wrote this poem in 1977. I set it to music after a retreat held in Rio de Janeiro, Brazil, before flying back to Paris. I finished it on the plane.

LOOKING FOR EACH OTHER

I have been looking for you, World Honored One,
since I was a little child.
With my first breath, I heard your call,
and began to look for you, Blessed One.
I've walked so many perilous paths,
confronted so many dangers,
endured despair, fear, hopes, and memories.
I've trekked to the farthest regions, immense and wild,
sailed the vast oceans,
traversed the highest summits, lost among the clouds.
I've lain dead, utterly alone,
on the sands of ancient deserts.
I've held in my heart so many tears of stone.

Blessed One, I've dreamed of drinking dewdrops
that sparkle with the light of far-off galaxies.
I've left footprints on celestial mountains
and screamed from the depths of Avici Hell, exhausted, crazed
    with despair
because I was so hungry, so thirsty.
For millions of lifetimes,
I've longed to see you,
but didn't know where to look.
Yet, I've always felt your presence with a mysterious certainty.

I know that for thousands of lifetimes,
you and I have been one,
and the distance between us is only a flash of thought.
Just yesterday while walking alone,
I saw the old path strewn with autumn leaves,

and the brilliant moon, hanging over the gate,
suddenly appeared like the image of an old friend.
And all the stars confirmed that you were there!
All night, the rain of compassion continued to fall,
while lightning flashed through my window
and a great storm arose,
as if Earth and Sky were in battle.
Finally in me the rain stopped, the clouds parted.
The moon returned,
shining peacefully, calming Earth and Sky.
Looking into the mirror of the moon, suddenly
I saw myself,
and I saw you smiling, Blessed One.
How strange!

The moon of freedom has returned to me,
everything I thought I had lost.
From that moment on,
and in each moment that followed,
I saw that nothing had gone.
There is nothing that should be restored.
Every flower, every stone, and every leaf recognize me.
Wherever I turn, I see you smiling
the smile of no-birth and no-death.
The smile I received while looking at the mirror of the moon.
I see you sitting there, solid as Mount Meru,
calm as my own breath,
sitting as though no raging fire storm ever occurred,
sitting in complete peace and in freedom.
At last I have found you, Blessed One,
and I have found myself.
There I sit.

The deep blue sky,
the snow-capped mountains painted against the horizon,
and the shining red sun sing with joy.
You, Blessed One, are my first love.
The love that is always present, always pure, and freshly new.
And I shall never need a love that will be called "last."
You are the source of well-being flowing through numberless
    troubled lives,
the water from your spiritual stream always pure, as it was in
    the beginning.
You are the source of peace,
solidity, and inner freedom.
You are the Buddha, the Tathagata.
With my one-pointed mind
I vow to nourish your solidity and freedom in myself
so I can offer solidity and freedom to countless others,
now and forever.

AT THE EDGE OF THE FOREST

(A Teacher Looking for His Student)

I have been looking for you, my child,
since rivers and mountains lay in obscurity.
I have been looking for you,
ever since life awaited the first rays of light.
I have been looking for you, as you lay in a long, deep sleep,
even as the conch echoed in the ten directions.
From the ancient mountain I cast my eyes across distant lands
and recognized your footprints on countless paths.

Where are you going?

There are times when, as the mist rises
and envelops a remote village,
I see you still wandering in faraway lands.
I call your name with every breath,
trusting that even though you have lost your way,
you will finally find a way back to me.
There are times I appear right on your path
but you still see me as a stranger.
You can't recognize our connection,
you can't remember the ancient vow cast in gold.
You can't recognize me,
so lost are you in dreams for a distant future.

In former lives, so many times you took my hand and we
    enjoyed walking together,
sitting for hours at the foot of centuries-old pines.
standing in silence,

listening to the wind softly calling us
as we gazed at white clouds floating by.
You picked up and offered me the first bright autumn leaf
and I took you through forests frozen deep in snow.
And yet wherever we went we always returned to our ancient
    mountain
to be close to the moon and stars
and to invite the great temple bell every morning to sound,
helping all beings to wake up.

We have sat quietly on An Tu Mountain with the Great
    Bamboo Forest Master
alongside frangipani trees in bloom;
we have taken ships out to rescue boat people drifting on the
    high seas;
we have helped Master Van Hanh design the Thang Long
    capital;
we have built a simple thatched hut,
and cast the net to rescue Trac Tuyen
as the tide roared along the banks of the Tien Duong river.
Together we have opened up the path and stepped
into the immensity of space outside of space,
after years of practicing to break free from the net of time.
We have harnessed the light of shooting stars
making a torch to guide people home
from years of wandering lost in endless striving.

And yet, when the vagabond seed in you springs back to life,
you abandon your teacher, you abandon your brothers and
    sisters,
and walk out, alone.
I behold you with compassion,

knowing that this is not a true separation, as I am already in
    every cell of your body.

Knowing that once again you need to play the prodigal child,
I promise to be there for you
every time you encounter hardship or danger.
When you find yourself unconscious on the hot sands of
    frontier deserts,
I manifest as a cloud to bring you cool shade.
In the depths of night the cloud condenses into dew,
a compassionate nectar falling drop by drop to revive you.
When you find yourself sitting in an abyss of darkness
utterly alienated from your true home,
I manifest as a long ladder gently descending
so you can climb up to the light
to discover again the vast blue sky
and the songs of brooks and birds.

There are times I have recognized you in Birmingham,
in the Gio Linh district or New England.
There are times I have met you in Hangzhou, Xiamen, or
    Shanghai.
There are times I have found you in St. Petersburg or East
    Berlin.
Even seeing you as a five-year-old child,
I recognize your true nature,
and the seed of bodhicitta in your young, tender heart.
Wherever I see you, I always raise
my hand to acknowledge you,
Whether in the delta of the North,
the city of Saigon, or the port of Thuan An.

There are times you have been the golden full moon
hanging above the peaks of Kim Son Mountain,
or the little bird calling
as it soars over the Dai Lao forest on a winter's night.
Many times I have seen you
but you have not seen me,
even though along your path the evening mist silently soaked
　　your clothes.
In the end you always come home.
You come home and sit at my feet on our ancient mountain,
as we listen to the birds calling, the monkeys hooting,
and the chant of morning prayer.
You come home to your teacher determined to be a vagabond
　　no more.

This morning the birds celebrate the rising sun.
Can you see, my child, that the white clouds still float in
　　freedom?
Where are you now?
The ancient mountain is still there in the heart of the present
　　moment,
even as the white-crested wave yearns to pull you toward
　　unknown shores.
Look again, and you will see me in you and in every leaf and
　　bud.
As soon as you call my name, you will see me right away.

Where are you going?

The old frangipani tree offers its fragrant flowers this morning.
You and I have never really been apart.
Spring has come.

The pines have put forth fresh green needles,
and at the edge of the forest,
the wild plum trees have burst into flower.

YOU SET OUT THIS MORNING

You set out this morning
to give the silver space a future.
The phoenix spreads her wings
and takes to the immense sky.
The water clings to the feet of the bridge,
while the sunrise calls for young birds.
The very place that served as a refuge for you years ago
is now witness to your departure
for the rivers and oceans of your homeland.

Paris, 1966

BECKONING

This morning's dawn
and I am here.
A cup of steaming tea,
a green lawn,
your sudden image from long ago,

your hands
or the wind
beckoning,
the shining of the tree's new bud.
Flower, leaf, and pebble—
all are chanting the *Lotus Sutra*.

*This poem was written in 1966 at a Catholic nunnery in Australia during
a speaking tour. I was sitting alone on the green grass, contemplating the
small buds, enjoying the lush vegetation, when a young nun brought me a
cup of tea. Then she went to the bell and said a prayer, holding the string
silently for some time before ringing the bell. I saw her as the archetypal
nun. After I wrote this poem, I offered it to her.*

THAT DISTANT AUTUMN MORNING

Seven years.
I can still feel the fragrance of sandalwood incense.
And your image, Mother,
is as vivid as ever.
It was an autumn morning,
sunny but cold.
You decided to go back
to the place you had come from.
Shaking the bodice of your long, worn-out dress,
you put down the heavy burden
of pain and sorrow.
I did not cry.

The world looked so strange.
You left with your heart still bleeding.
My monk's robe was caressed by the morning wind.
The sunshine was a golden color.
The sky was blue.
The hills were high.
And there was your small earthen grave, newly made.
When the few who had stayed behind with me left,
I talked to you alone about life.
My heart was broken,
but I was at peace.

You suffered, Mother,
and existence weighed too heavily on your shoulders.

Seven years.
Since then you have come back to me many times,

and each time so alive.
Today I shed a tear for you of remembrance and compassion.
I want to share your sorrow
with the heart of a child.
Existence still on my shoulders,
I go back to that autumn morning,
that distant autumn morning,
filled with the fragrance of sandalwood incense.
You see, I am now on that high hill,
embraced by the bright sunshine.

Do stay with me the whole day, Mother.
I do not know where the events of life will bring me tomorrow,
but I know you are truly here.
My true love,
I want to cry silently,
my head covered in my two arms,
every time I go back to the sweet motherland of childhood.

I wrote this poem seven years after my mother passed away. Three years before, I had had a dream in which I saw my mother—young, vivid, joyful, and beautiful, with long black hair. Waking up at midnight, I went out to the moonlit garden and discovered that my mother had never died. This happened while I stayed at the Bao Loc Temple in the highlands of Central Vietnam.

CALM

Childhood—
sunny age of twelve—
what do you say?

Ancient river
old town
clouds call to a blue sky

calm

DISAPPEARANCE

The leaf-tips bend
under the weight of dew.
Fruits are ripening
in Earth's early morning.
Daffodils light up in the sun.
The curtain of cloud at the gateway
of the garden path begins to shift:
have pity for childhood,
the way of illusion.

Late at night,
the candle gutters.
In some distant desert,
a flower opens.
And somewhere else,
a cold aster
that never knew a cassava patch
or gardens of areca palms,
never knew the joy of life,
at that instant disappears—
man's eternal yearning.

Written around 1966.

DROPS OF EMPTINESS

My heart is cooled
by drops of emptiness.
Suddenly I see
my boat has crossed the river
and reached the shore of non-yearning.
Soft sand, empty beach,
old promises . . .

Written around 1966.

JOURNEY

Here are words written down—
footprints on the sand,
cloud formations.

Tomorrow
I'll be gone.

ILLUSION TRANSFORMED

Horizon's heavy eyelids,
mountains leaning,
seeking rest from Earth's pillow—
at nightfall
grass and flowers perfume sleep.

Illusion shifts her veils.

Wind lifts up her hands.
Jade candles
shimmer in the silver river of the sky.
The hillside's open doorway
frames a falling star that writes
the sacred words in fire.
Ten thousand lives are spinning,
circling dream's illusion.
The moment of this night
reveals
this world's reality.

Written in the Fontvannes hermitage, 1970.

MOVEMENT

My head pillowed on waves—
I drift with the flow—
broad river,
deep sky.
They float, they sink,
like bubbles,
like wings.

1966.

THE AFTERNOON RIVER AND
THE EARTH'S SOUL

Trees by the river,
riverside streets,
blue sky,
blue leaves,
a high-roofed temple.

The soul of the tower
sleeps
on this calm,
Sunday afternoon.

From afar,
vaguely,
I hear
Earth's soul—
lonely,
when the stars' festival
is in full swing.

*I wrote this in Paris in 1967, after walking along the Seine River on a
Sunday afternoon.*

THE VIRTUOUS MAN

The two leaves of the pinewood gate fall shut.

A shimmering arrow leaves the bow,
speeds upward, splits the sky,
and explodes the sun.

The blossoms of the orange trees fall
until the courtyard is carpeted—

flickering reflection
of infinity.

Paris, 1967.

PADMAPANI

Flowers in the sky.
Flowers on Earth.
Lotuses bloom as Buddha's eyelids.
Lotuses bloom in man's heart.
Holding gracefully a lotus in his hand,
the bodhisattva brings forth a universe of art.
In the meadows of the sky, stars have sprung up.
The smiling, fresh moon is already up.
The jade-colored trunk of a coconut tree
reaches across the late-night sky.

My mind, traveling in utmost emptiness,
catches suchness on its way home.

I wrote this poem after visiting the Ajanta Caves in India in 1976.

LANKA

The island has been lullabied for thousands of years by the
    ocean.
The sounds of the waves express the deepest love.
Water-buffalo boys walk the beach with their bare feet,
their skin smelling of the good smell of the ocean.
All the sails this morning are filled with wind.
Rows of coconut trees shelter and nourish the perfumed earth.
Bananas, jackfruits, mangoes, and papayas are as sweet as ever.
On the high pass over the mountain, it rains very hard.
The wind blows fiercely,
but the footprints of Lord Buddha remain intact.
The glorious morning comes, a festival day.
The sounds of a drum escort the music.
Young ladies of the countryside
celebrate the coming of the Buddha—
their richly decorated brown feet
touching the Earth with joyful, gracious dances.

Written in Sri Lanka, 1976.

STRANGE SHORES

Attempts are made to catch space
and release it again.
Colors try to share light,
and a carpet of clouds unrolls under my feet.
Down a deserted path, I see through my soul
and the true face of former lives reveals itself
in the present moment.
Because the window of time is open,
the curtain of reminiscence floats in the wind,
in the sunshine, and in the green color.

I see a permanent spring
atop the Himalayan range.
There is a meadow no one has seen,
where the grass is always fresh.
Here and there in the sky, stars appear
like little golden and violet flowers.
The man bites on his finger to concentrate.
My boat has just landed on a strange shore,
completely silent under the light of the stars.
A child is talking.
Is that a familiar world?
Listen.

My soul continues its flight.
Permission has not been granted.
The captain found his arms tightly bound by the string of time.
Suddenly I hear the murmur of the wind.
The great bird has just spread its immense wings.
Space is now entirely yours!

Where are you going?
A distant star is calling.
Although the planet feels at a loss,
the sky and the clouds still appear friendly.
The fog rises on the surface of the river.
Evening clouds gather.

Waiting for me over there
are my mother and younger brother.
At noontime,
the perfume of areca blossoms
and the sound of grinding hamoc
suggest that you need some lunch.
I remain in my seat and feel sleepy.
Out there, the moon is also leaning on a mountain.
Who are you, young man?
This morning it happened that we got to know each other.
Now he is leaning his head on a cushion.
The thinking is like a long thread.
The silkworm uses her silky substance
to build up a prison for herself.
The wind continues to murmur in my ears.
A small biscuit,
a tiny cup of coffee.
I found myself half-awakened.

The air hostess walks as if on a cloud.

MIND'S MOON

Excitedly, the sky celebrates a new sunset.
The bird with eyes reflecting the color of the sky
hops around branches
and leaves made of crystal.
Waking up from a long sleep,
I find dawn rising in me,
and in the pond of the mind, a peaceful moon reflecting itself.
The butterfly is out of its homeland.
The violet tía tô leaves
announce the ripening of autumn.
Birds sing in the leaves.
Sky and clouds are peaceful.
This morning is peace.
The dove spreads her wings.
The child opens her arms
for a heartfelt welcoming.
The birds welcome drops of new sunshine.
Golden is the color of the lawn.

It has been ten years
since the butterfly wandered from its homeland.

CAO PHONG

The news came yesterday from the warmth of the Earth.
At midnight, from the continent,
a source of fragrant milk suddenly springs forth in abundance.
The splendid moment arrives
when the sun makes its appearance
on the top of the high mountain.

Written for Cao Phong ("High Peak") upon receiving the news of his birth.

ARMFULS OF POETRY,
DROPS OF SUNSHINE

Sunshine rides on space and poetry on sunshine.
Poetry gives birth to sunshine, and sunshine to poetry.

Sun treasured in the heart of the bitter melon,
poetry made of steam rising from a bowl of soup in winter.
The wind is lurking outside, swirling.
Poetry is back to haunt the old hills and prairies.
Yet the poor thatched hut remains on the river shore, waiting.

Spring carries poetry in its drizzle.
The fire sparkles poetry in its orange flame.

Sunshine stored in the heart of the fragrant wood,
warm smoke leading poetry back to the pages
of an unofficial history book.
Sunshine, though absent from space,
fills the now rose-colored stove.

Sunshine reaching out takes the color of smoke;
poetry in its stillness, the color of the misty air.

Spring rain holds poetry in its drops
which bend down to kiss the soil,
so that the seeds may sprout.
Following the rain, poetry comes to dwell on each leaf.
Sunshine has a green color, and poetry a pink one.
Bees deliver warmth to the flowers from the sunshine
they carry on their wings.

On sunshine footsteps to the deep forest,
poetry drinks the nectar with joy.
With the excitement of celebration,
butterflies and bees crowd the Earth.
Sunshine makes up the dance, and poetry the song.

Drops of sweat fall on the hard ground.
Poems fly along the furrows.
The hoe handily on my shoulder, poetry flows from the breath.
Sunshine wanes away down the river,
and the silhouette of the late afternoon lingers reluctantly.
Poetry is leaving for the horizon
where the King of Light is blanketing himself in clouds.

A green sun found in a basketful of fresh vegetables,
a tasty and well-cooked sun smells delicious in a bowl of rice.
Poetry looks with a child's eyes.
Poetry feels with a weather-beaten face.
Poetry stays within each attentive look.
Poetry—the hands that work the poor and arid land
    somewhere far away.

The smiling sun brightening up the sunflower;
the ripe and full sun hiding itself in an August peach;
poetry follows each meditative step,
poetry lines up the pages.

Discreetly,
within closed food packages,
poetry nurtures love.

This poem, translated from the Vietnamese by Hoang Thi Van, has a lot of interbeing in it. The sun is green, because you can recognize it in the vegetables. Poetry is born from the wood that is burning in the stove. Without it, I cannot write. The last lines of the poem speak about the work of helping hungry children. We have used this poem as a New Year's greeting.

IN THE FOREST

The community of trees—
thousands of bodies
with a human body among them.
Branches and leaves are waving.
Then the call of the creek,
and my eyes open to the sky of the great Mind.
A smile is seen
on every leaf.

The forest is here,
because the city is down there.
But Mind has gone with the trees
and put on a new green dress.

The sunshine is the leaves.
The leaves are the sunshine.
The sunshine is no different from the leaves.
The leaves are no different from the sunshine.
All other forms and sounds
are of the same nature.

ONENESS

The moment I die,
I will try to come back to you
as quickly as possible.
I promise it will not take long.
Isn't it true
I am already with you,
as I die each moment?
I come back to you
in every moment.
Just look,
feel my presence.
If you want to cry,
please cry.
And know
that I will cry with you.
The tears you shed
will heal us both.
Your tears are mine.
The earth I tread this morning
transcends history.
Spring and winter are both present in the moment.
The young leaf and the dead leaf are really one.
My feet touch deathlessness,
and my feet are yours.
Walk with me now.
Let us enter the dimension of oneness
and see the cherry tree blossom in winter.
Why should we talk about death?
I don't need to die
to be back with you.

ONE ARROW, TWO ILLUSIONS

The river winds its way to the sea.
Tomorrow, when it is time for you to depart,
I will ask you to sing aloud
your song of the new season.
The echo of your voice will soothe
and guide me on my way
at least for some distance.

In fact, I will never depart.
Even if I could, I would arrive nowhere.
The moment I depart, if there is such a thing,
there are moons, clouds, winds, and rivers.
And at the moment of arrival,
there will also be violet bamboos and yellow chrysanthemums.

A leaf,
a flower—
that is what you are.
That is why we have been together
since the no-beginning.
There is no way I could not be with you.
Still you don't understand,
and you keep asking me about my departure.

This morning, as the moon and stars return
from their deep sleep,
Earth is pretending to weep.
She has shed so many tears.
You, too, should weep, my dear.
Your tears will be like crystals. (Weeping makes you beautiful.)

Your tears will transform the deserts into green gardens,
refreshing the Earth, ushering in buds of hope.

When we were children, I longed to weep
each time I saw you weeping.
The smile of the Earth,
our mother with green hair,
brings birds and butterflies to leaves and flowers.
We have never been born.
Look back at your true mind.

The day when I arose from the hidden dimension,
my image was revealed to you
through the five elements.
But that image will soon disappear,
and you will have to look for me
in what has not yet come
and cannot depart.
Looking for me,
looking for yourself,
will be a joy!
You will find yourself in the non-coming and non-going.
With one arrow,
you will bring down two illusions—
finding the non-coming and non-going amidst samsara,
water amidst waves.

My smile this morning
is to bring you the everlasting spring.
Be the Tathagata.
Be one with the smile.

The day when you pierce through illusion,
you will also find that smile.
Nothing remains, and yet nothing will be lost.
This morning the birds and the springs beckon,
"Continue singing, my little flower."

This poem is about you and your Dharma brother or sister, and about life and death. Your brother loves you so much that he is afraid of losing you. Thinking that you may disappear or die in the situation of war and social injustice as a compassionate worker, he asks you to leave something behind that he can hold onto as he continues down the path. This is the big brother's answer: "I have never been born. I will never die. If you are able to see me in my nature of no-birth and no-death, then you can also see your own nature of no-birth and no-death." With one arrow, you can bring down two illusions—his nonbeing and your nonbeing. This poem was banned by both the North and the South during the war. They thought that it was a plea for a neutral Vietnam, neither communist nor capitalist.

THE OLD MENDICANT

Being rock, being gas, being mist, being Mind,
being the mesons traveling among the galaxies
at the speed of light,
you have come here, my beloved.
And your blue eyes shine, so beautiful, so deep.
You have taken the path traced for you
from the non-beginning and the never-ending.
You say that on your way here
you have gone through
many millions of births and deaths.
Innumerable times you have been transformed
into fire storms in outer space.
You have used your own body
to measure the age of the mountains and rivers.
You have manifested yourself
as trees, grass, butterflies, single-celled beings,
and as chrysanthemums.
But the eyes with which you look at me this morning
tell me that you have never died.
Your smile invites me into the game
whose beginning no one knows,
the game of hide-and-seek.

O green caterpillar, you are solemnly using your body
to measure the length of the rose branch that grew last summer.
Everyone says that you, my beloved, were just born this spring.
Tell me, how long have you been around?
Why wait until this moment to reveal yourself to me,
carrying with you that smile which is so silent and so deep?
O caterpillar, suns, moons, and stars flow out

each time I exhale.
Who knows that the infinitely large must be found
in your tiny body?
Upon each point on your body,
thousands of Buddha fields have been established.
With each stretch of your body, you measure time
from the non-beginning to the never-ending.
The great mendicant of old is still there on Vulture Peak,
contemplating the ever-splendid sunset.

Gautama, how strange!
Who said that the Udumbara flower blooms
only once every 3,000 years?

The sound of the rising tide—you cannot help hearing it
if you have an attentive ear.

This "love poem," as Joanna Macy calls it, has to do with the original face. In Buddhism, when a teacher says to his student, "Show me your original face," it is an invitation to discover one's nature of interbeing. "My beloved, you have come from the mineral, the gas, the mist, and consciousness. You have gone through many galaxies at the speed of light. And no-beginning and no-ending have come together in order to trace your way. And now you are a caterpillar. I look into you and I recognize that. Although you look small, you have created a fire storm in outer space. And you have measured the age of river and mountains with your tiny body." The infinitely small contains the infinitely large. Practicing meditation is like seeking your beloved. The old mendicant, Shakyamuni Buddha, is still sitting there. Don't think that he has disappeared. He is still contemplating the beautiful sunset. His preaching is still strong, like the sound of the rising tide, if you have ears to hear it.

I first visited Vulture Peak in 1968, and once in the early evening I saw myself contemplating the sunset with the eyes of the Buddha. When a group of us went there together in 1988, I felt the same thing again. This poem was written in 1970.

APPARITION

Being young
is like sweet sunshine
flooding the summer sky.

Quiet noon—
Years and months
are just the expressions of Earth.

Why take note
of the never-ending seasons?

Paris, 1966.

THE STORY OF A RIVER

Born on the top of a mountain, the little spring dances her way down. The stream of water sings as she travels. She wants to go fast. She is unable to go slowly. Running, rushing, is the only way, maybe even flying. She wants to arrive. Arrive where? Arrive at the ocean. She has heard of the deep, blue, beautiful ocean. To become one with the ocean, that is what she wants.

Coming down to the plains, she grows into a young river. Winding her way through the beautiful meadows, she has to slow down. "Why can't I run the way I could when I was a creek? I want to reach the deep, blue ocean. If I continue this slowly, how will I ever arrive there at all?" As a creek, she was not happy with what she was. She really wanted to grow into a river. But, as a river, she does not feel happy either. She cannot bear to slow down.

Then, as she slows down, the young river begins to notice the beautiful clouds reflected in her water. They are of different colors and shapes floating in the sky, and they seem to be free to go anywhere they please. Wanting to be like a cloud, she begins to chase after the clouds, one after another. "I am not happy as a river. I want to be like you, or I shall suffer. Life is really not worth living."

So the river begins to play the game. She chases after clouds. She learns to laugh and cry. But the clouds do not stay in one place for very long. "They reflect themselves in my water, but then they leave. No cloud seems to be faithful. Every cloud I know has left me. No cloud has ever brought me satisfaction or happiness. I hate their betrayal." The excitement of chasing after clouds is not worth the suffering and despair.

One afternoon, a strong wind carried all the clouds away. The sky became desperately empty. There were no more clouds to chase after. Life became empty for the river. She was so lonely she didn't want to live anymore. But how could a river die? From something you become nothing? From someone, you become no one? Is it possible?

During the night, the river went back to herself. She could not sleep. She listened to her own cries, the lapping of her water against the shore. This was the first time she had ever listened deeply to herself, and in doing so, she discovered something very important: her water was made of clouds. She had been chasing after clouds and she did not know that clouds were her own nature. The river realized that the object of her search was within her. She touched peace. Suddenly, she could stop. She no longer felt the need to run after something outside herself. She was already what she wanted to become. The peace she experienced was truly gratifying and brought her a deep rest, a deep sleep.

When the river woke up the next morning, she discovered something new and wonderful reflected in her water—the blue sky. "How deep it is, how calm. The sky is immense, stable, welcoming, and utterly free." It seemed impossible to believe that this was the first time the river ever reflected the sky in her water. But that is true, because in the past, she was interested only in the clouds, and she never paid attention to the sky. No cloud could ever leave the sky. She knew that the clouds were there, hidden somewhere in the blue sky. The sky must contain within itself all the clouds and all the waters. Clouds seem impermanent, but the sky is always there as the faithful home of all the clouds.

Touching the sky, the river touched stability. She touched the ultimate. In the past, she had only touched the coming, going, being, and nonbeing of the clouds. Now she was able to touch the home of all coming, going, being, and nonbeing. No one could take the sky out of her water anymore. How wonderful it was to stop and touch! The stopping and touching brought her true stability and peace. She had arrived home.

That afternoon, the wind ceased to blow. The clouds came back one by one. The river had become wise. She was able to welcome each cloud with a smile. The clouds of many colors and shapes seemed to be the same, but then again they were no longer the same for the river. She did not feel the need to possess or chase after any particular cloud. She smiled to each cloud with equanimity and loving kindness. She enjoyed their reflections in her water. But when they drifted away, the river did not feel deserted. She waved to them, saying, "Good-bye. Have a nice journey." She was no longer bound to any of the clouds.

The day was a happy one. That night, when the river calmly opened up her heart to the sky, she received the most wonderful image ever reflected in her water—a beautiful full moon, a moon so bright, refreshing, smiling.

The full moon of the Buddha travels
in the sky of utmost emptiness.
If the rivers of living beings are calm,
the refreshing moon will reflect
beautifully in their water.

All space seemed to be there for the enjoyment of the moon, and she looked utterly free. The river reflected the moon in her water and enjoyed the same freedom and happiness.

What a wonderful, festive night for everyone—the sky, clouds, moon, stars, and water. In the boundless space, sky, clouds, moon, stars, and water enjoyed walking in meditation together. They walked with no need to arrive anywhere, not even the ocean. They could just be happy in the present moment. The river did not need to arrive at the ocean to become water. She knew she was water by nature and at the same time a cloud, the moon, the sky, the stars, and the snow. Why should she run away from herself? Who speaks of a river as not flowing? A river does flow, yes. But she does not need to rush.

INTERBEING

The sun has entered me.
The sun has entered me together with the cloud and the river.
I myself have entered the river,
and I have entered the sun
with the cloud and the river.
There has not been a moment
when we do not interpenetrate.

But before the sun entered me,
the sun was in me—
also the cloud and the river.
Before I entered the river,
I was already in it.
There has not been a moment
when we have not inter-been.

Therefore you know
that as long as you continue to breathe,
I continue to be in you.

LOVE POEM

Your eyes are made of the six elements—
earth, water, fire, air,
space, and consciousness.
They are made of these only,
but they are beautiful.
Should I make them mine?
Should I try to make them last for a long time?
Should I try to record them?
But I know that what I can record
would not be your true eyes.

Your voice is made of the six elements,
but it is truly lovely.
Should I try to make it mine?
Should I record it?
But I know that what I can hold on to or record
would not be your true voice.
What I get may only be a picture,
a magnetic tape,
a painting,
or a book.

Your smile is made of the six elements,
but it is truly wonderful.
Should I try to make it mine?
Should I try to make it last for a long time?
Should I try to own or record it?
But I know that what I can own or record
could not be your true smile.
It would only be some of the elements.

Your eyes are impermanent.
Your eyes are not you.
Yes, I have been told,
and I have seen it,
yet they are still beautiful.

Just because they are impermanent,
they are all the more beautiful.
The things that do not last long
are the most beautiful things—
a shooting star, a firework.

Just because they are without a self,
they are all the more beautiful.
What does a self have to do with beautiful eyes?

I want to contemplate your beautiful eyes,
even if I know
that they do not last
even if I know
they do not have a self.

Your eyes are beautiful.
I am aware that they are impermanent.
But what is wrong with impermanence?
Without impermanence, could anything exist at all?

Your eyes are beautiful.
I am told that they are not you, they have no self.
But what is wrong with the nature of nonself?
With self, could anything be there at all?

So although your eyes are only made of the six elements,
although they are impermanent,
although they are not you,
they are still beautiful,
and I want to contemplate them.
I want to enjoy looking at them as long as they are available.

Knowing your eyes are impermanent,
I enjoy them without trying to make them last forever,
without trying to hold on to or record them
or make them mine.
Loving your eyes, I remain free.

Loving your eyes,
I learn to love them deeply.
I see the six elements which they are,
the six wonderful elements.
These elements are so beautiful.
And I learn to love them too.

There are so many things I love—
your eyes, the blue sky,
your voice, the birds in the trees,
your smile, and the butterflies on the flowers.
I learn each moment
to be a better lover.
I learn each moment
to discover my true love.

Your eyes are beautiful.
So is your voice, your smile,
the sky,

the birds,
the butterflies.
I love them. I vow to protect them. Yes.
I know to love is to respect.
And reverence
is the nature of my love.

INTERRELATIONSHIP

You are me, and I am you.
Isn't it obvious that we "inter-are"?
You cultivate the flower in yourself,
so that I will be beautiful.
I transform the garbage in myself,
so that you will not have to suffer.

I support you;
you support me.
I am in this world to offer you peace;
you are in this world to bring me joy.

1989. Written during a retreat for psychotherapists held in Colorado in response to Fritz Perls' statement, "You are you, and I am me, and if by chance we meet, that's wonderful. If not, it couldn't be helped."

YOU ARE MY GARDEN

A tree is dying in my garden.
You see it,
but you also see other trees
that are still vigorous and joyful.

And I am thankful.

I know a tree is dying in my garden,
but I do not see it
as the whole of my garden.

And I need you to remind me of that.

I am told to take care of the garden
left to me by my ancestors.
A garden always has beautiful trees
and others that are not so healthy.
That is the reason why
we have to take good care of it.

You are my garden,
and I know that I should practice as a gardener.

I have seen an old, untended garden,
where the cherry and peach trees
still bloom wonderfully
and always in time.

DEFUSE ME

If I were a bomb
ready to explode,
if I have become
dangerous to your life,
then you must take care of me.
You think you can get away from me,
but how?
I am here, right in your midst.
(You cannot remove me from your life.)
And I may explode
at any time.
I need your care.
I need your time.
I need you to defuse me.
You are responsible for me,
because you have made the vow (and I heard it)
to love and to care.

I know that to take care of me
you need much patience,
much coolness.
I realize that in you
there is also a bomb to be defused.
So why don't we help each other?

I need you to listen to me.
No one has listened to me.
No one understands my suffering,
including the ones who say they love me.
The pain inside me

is suffocating me.
It is the TNT
that makes up the bomb.
There is no one else
who will listen to me.
That is why I need you.
But you seem to be getting away from me.
You want to run for your safety,
the kind of safety
that does not exist.

I have not created my own bomb.
It is you.
It is society.
It is family.
It is school.
It is tradition.
So please don't blame me for it.
Come and help;
if not, I will explode.
This is not a threat.
It is only a plea for help.
I will also be of help
when it is your turn.

WE WILL BE BACK AGAIN

One will be three.
One will be four.
One will be a thousand.
We'll be back again.
We'll be back again.

Here is the rushing of the rain,
and the vast ocean of the Mind.
I am riding splendidly on this towering wave—
hills and mountains, hills and mountains,
oceans and rivers, oceans and rivers—
the wings of the albatross are playing with the morning sunlight.

Are snow and light the same thing?
Let the song be continued on the lips of the child!

Sometimes people become two (if they get married) or three (if they have a child). Usually we think that rebirth means one person will continue as one person. But one person may become several, just as one kernel of corn, when reborn, becomes an ear of corn with many kernels. The extraordinary thing is that I first met you as one person, but now when you come back, you are three or five. The most important thing is that joy and freedom be always there. I do not mind if you come back as a multitude. But be sure to come back with joy and freedom.

FULL MOON FESTIVAL

What will happen when form collides with emptiness,
and what will happen when perception enters
    non-perception?
Come here with me, friend.
Let's watch together.
Do you see the two clowns, life and death
setting up a play on a stage?
Here comes autumn.
The leaves are ripe.
Let the leaves fly.
A festival of colors, yellow, red.
The branches have held on to the leaves
during spring and summer.
This morning they let them go.
Flags and lanterns are displayed.
Everyone is here at the Full Moon Festival.

Friend, what are you waiting for?
The bright moon shines above us.
There are no clouds tonight.
Why bother to ask about lamps and fire?
Why talk about cooking dinner?
Who is searching and who is finding?
Let us just enjoy the moon, all night.

*This poem is written in response to Vietnamese Dhyana master Lieu Quan
(1670–1742), whose poem of insight has this sentence: "If I had realized
that the lamp is fire itself, the rice would have been cooked for a long time
already!" The insight poem was presented to his teacher, Master Tu Dung,
in 1708.*

NON-DUALITY

The bell tolls at four in the morning.
I stand by the window,
barefoot on the cool floor.
The garden is still dark.
I wait for the mountains and rivers to reclaim their shapes.
There is no light in the deepest hours of the night.
Yet, I know you are there
in the depth of the night,
the immeasurable world of the mind.
You, the known, have been there
ever since the knower has been.

The dawn will come soon,
and you will see
that you and the rosy horizon
are within my two eyes.
It is for me that the horizon is rosy
and the sky blue.
Looking at your image in the clear stream,
you answer the question by your very presence.
Life is humming the song of the non-dual marvel.
I suddenly find myself smiling
in the presence of this immaculate night.
I know because I am here that you are there,
and your being has returned to show itself
in the wonder of tonight's smile.
In the quiet stream,
I swim gently.
The murmur of the water lulls my heart.
A wave serves as a pillow.

I look up and see
a white cloud against the blue sky,
the sound of autumn leaves,
the fragrance of hay—
each one a sign of eternity.
A bright star helps me find my way back to myself.

I know because you are there that I am here.
The stretching arm of cognition
in a lightning flash,
joining together a million eons of distance,
joining together birth and death,
joining together the known and the knower.

In the depth of the night,
as in the immeasurable realm of consciousness,
the garden of life and I
remain each other's objects.
The flower of being is singing the song of emptiness.

The night is still immaculate,
but sounds and images from you
have returned and fill the pure night.
I feel their presence.
By the window, with my bare feet on the cool floor,
I know I am here
for you to be.

This poem was written in 1964 at the Bamboo Grove Temple (Truc Lam)
in Go Vap, Gia Dinh. Upon returning to Vietnam, I set up the Institute of
Higher Buddhist Studies; published a weekly, Hai Triêu Am (The Sound
of the Rising Tide); *and prepared the ground for founding the School of*

Youth for Social Service. I would go back to that temple very often to enjoy the calm and beautiful atmosphere there, because the Institute of Higher Buddhist Studies was in the center of the city.

One morning in my little hut, I woke up very early, around three o'clock. When I put my feet on the earthen floor, the coolness made me feel very awake. I remained in that position for about fifty minutes. I listened to the first bells of the morning, while I looked out into the darkness. Although I could not distinguish particular objects, I knew that the plum tree and the bamboo thicket were there. In the darkness of the night, I knew that you were there, because I was there. The subject of consciousness is, therefore the object of consciousness must be.

This poem is about an insight related to vijñanavada. It is a difficult poem, fit to be explained in a course on vijñanavada. You are there for me, and I am here for you. That is the teaching of interbeing. The term interbeing was not yet used at that time. Although we think of the Avatamsaka when we hear the term interbeing, the teaching of interbeing also has its roots in vijñanavada, because in vijñanavada, cognition always includes subject and object together. Consciousness is always consciousness of something.

VOYAGE

The wind is silent this noontime,
and four cypresses stand in line.
The wall shows its bones—
erosion, water of time.

The blue sky is calm.
I find myself here to discover the age
of the bricks and stones
that have patiently waited,
for millions of years.

My flesh and bones
in their journey through the desert
make a quick stop here
and leave a little warmth from the palm of my hand,
a bit of the rhythm of the heart.

The ancient image is far away,
but you are still here waiting.

Tell me,
did I stop here once during a previous existence?
I find myself looking for my footprints
left during one cycle of birth and death.

Which atoms will be dancing
in the small space of my palm
someday when the five elements of man
return to their source?

Whose dead body lies by this wall
this summer noontime
while the sky smiles its blue smile?

O bricks and stones,
who will go
and who will stay?
I would carry all of you with me
 in the same voyage at the same speed.
You who have sought to find the going and coming—
tell me, where is the line of the horizon?

I can see now
that all of us
since the beginning of time
have been flowing at the same speed.
Give me enough time to call back
the starfruit and acacias of the ancient years.

Together with the four cypresses today,
we have stopped for a moment
to contemplate the wondrous trip.
Although this calm blue sky has been here a million eons,
it is only to me now that this blue sky has just been born.

*I was alone on the French Riviera, working on my book on the myths of
Vietnam,* A Taste of Earth. *I went to the beach and sat there without
thinking or doing anything for a whole day, until ten o'clock at night.
I allowed my five* skandhas *to be washed by the sound and sight of the
waves. Then I went to Provence, where I found myself beside a very old
wall and four cypresses standing in a line. And I saw my dead body lying
by the old wall.*

This poem is about a trip. All of us are on a journey, but we go at different speeds. From time to time, you may recognize something familiar in what you see for the first time. You know you are seeing that person or thing for the first time, but you have the distinct impression you have met before. My interpretation is that you have met already while orbiting the same star, but because you went too fast, you overtook the other person or thing, and now you meet again. Stones and bricks may go at a slower speed. When I climbed up to Heidelberg Castle in Germany, I had the impression that it was not for the first time. This moved me to write the poem, "The Song of No Coming and No Going." Insight is something like the blue sky: it has always been there, but it looks as though it is just being born.

STOPPING THE WHEEL

Who is going through samsara?
If we are to stop samsara,
whose samsara is to be stopped?

Afflictions and pains are going through samsara,
and we are to stop them from continuing the circle.

But who is the one who shoulders these afflictions and pains?
Afflictions do not need someone to shoulder them.
They go through samsara by themselves.

What will happen after samsara is stopped?
Samsara will happen again.
Why bother to stop it?
When the samsara wheel of ill-being stops,
the samsara wheel of well-being begins to turn.

The stopping of ill-being starts the beginning of well-being,
but well-being is still samsara.
Well-being needs to go through samsara,
because we always need it
in each moment of our life.

Why should you want the smile of the little boy to be absent?
Why should we ban the breeze of spring?
Ending samsara
is transforming suffering,
and suffering is the substance
which makes up happiness.

Don't worry too much, my friend.
Even suffering is needed in this world.

MOON VIEWING

If there is no self,
there will be no samsara.
Why then do you have to dissolve the self?
Why do you have to stop samsara?

There is no self,
but there is the belief in a self.
There is no samsara,
but there is the idea of samsara.

Is the full moon tonight a self?
No, it is not a self.
Is the moon viewer a self?
No, he is not a self.

How then can the moon viewer enjoy the moon?
It is precisely because the moon has no self
and the moon viewer has no self
that both moon and moon viewer are wonderful,
and that moon viewing is a wonderful thing.

Moon viewing is our practice.

SUNFLOWER

Come, dear, with your innocent eyes
and look at the clear, blue ocean of the Dharmakaya,
and look at the green color,
the manifestation of suchness.

Even if the world is shattered,
your smile will never vanish.
What did we possess yesterday,
and what will we lose today?

Come, dear, look right into existence,
adorned by illusion.
Since the sunflower is already there,
all flowers turn toward it and contemplate.

The sunflower is prajñaparamita, *transcendent understanding.*

[UNTITLED]

Listen to the call of the homeland.
Mountains and rivers are so beautiful.
Let us go back to our home to touch our roots.
Crossing the bridges of understanding and love,
we arrive at our true home.

BIRTH AND DEATH

During many lifetimes, birth and death are present,
giving rise to birth and death.
The moment the notion of birth and death arises,
birth and death are there.
As soon as the notion of birth and death dies,
real life is born.

This poem was written in 1974, during a conference organized by the World Council of Churches in Sri Lanka. The original is a repetition of only two Chinese characters (sheng: life, or to be born, and si: death, or to die) arranged in such a way that they produce the meaning seen in the above translation.

> *sheng sheng sheng si sheng*
> *si sheng sheng si sheng*
> *si sheng sheng sheng si*
> *si sheng si sheng sheng*

THE GREAT LION'S ROAR

White clouds float.
Tuong vi roses bloom.
The ones that float are clouds.
The ones that bloom are roses.
A tuong vi rose blooms,
and a white cloud floats.

There would be no cloud if there were no floating.
There would be no flower if there were no blooming.
The cloud is itself the floating,
and the flower the blooming.
Mental constructions and the formation of words,
figures, and concepts
have opened up the maze.

The point is only the meeting point
of two lines that seek each other.
A line is a point that moves.
I build the high with the low.
I establish the low with the high.
I establish the left with the right.
I divide the many with the one.
My hand has five fingers,
long ones and short ones.
They are branches carrying young leaves.
My thoughts grow like flower buds
blooming on the trees.

My body is a tree
of blood, flesh, bones, and saliva
cells and nerves,
figures and images,
food and waste.
Here are bones
that will remain tomorrow.
They are not mine.
They are not yours.
But, Oh, compassion,
they give the illusion of permanence and non-permanence,
making you cry silently from time to time
for the destiny of man.

My thoughts—
I send them off
in ten directions on the waves of communication.
You find ways to record them.
Words that I utter, waves of sound,
repeatedly transmit themselves.
You find ways to record them.
My images are projected.
My lips move when I speak.
My eyes smile.
You find ways to record them,
thinking that you can preserve them.
Along the line of time and space,
you try to find the marks
that replace the real.
I show you the film.
Your fingers touch the images on the screen.

Compassion,
compassion for whom?

At the British Museum that day,
a man lay on his left side,
with the marks of anxiety imprinted on his forehead.
Three thousand years before Christ,
three thousand after Christ—
what is the difference?
We say that the hot sand preserved him,
like that tape recorder.
What can the hot sand preserve
but a marvelous
message of pain?
My flesh is warm, tender.
The blood runs in my veins peacefully.
There are endocrine glands
that are not yet dried up.
There is sperm and saliva,
a fresh, lovely smile,
and desires, hopes, and projects.

I have at times embraced
life in my two arms—
a red balloon
in the arms of a young country boy.

Because the blood is not yet dried up,
because the sperm is not yet dried up,
to be, of course, is a marvelous thing.
Not to be is also a marvelous thing.
To be and not to be are in fact the same.

Only the illusion about it
creates the sensation of pain.
To be or not to be is not truly the question.

My flesh is tender today.
My nerves vibrate—
the mattress on the bed of life, warm and soft.
I hear the sound of wailing.
O, superb colors and forms—
they are there, because my eyes are there.
O wondrous sounds—
they are there, because my ears are there.
Being superb and wondrous
is being superb and wondrous for this manas.
To have manas is a wondrous thing.
Not to have manas is also a wondrous thing.
Being wondrous is being wondrous.
Manas, O manas.

Being is the being of manas.
Nonbeing is the nonbeing of manas.
Being wondrous is being or nonbeing.
Is manas a being or a nonbeing?
Manas, O manas;
No-manas, O, no-manas.
Both manas and no-manas
are simply manas.
Both being and nonbeing have been invented.
Manas, let me laugh aloud.

I stamped my feet and cried
the moment mother died.

That morning was a beautiful rosy morning,
but at midnight the wind blew hard.
Tears ran silently down my cheeks.
The tears preserved in the glands
are enough for a whole winter.
My mother smiling,
my mother not smiling—
Did mother exist or not?
I stamped my feet.
The soil gives way under my feet
and creates in my footprints a real emptiness.

Yesterday the sunshine was mild.
Mother grew a few beds of flowers.
She died at midnight.
Lush plants grow and flowers smile.
"Don't smile, you naughty flowers."
"My goodness! How funny this fellow is."

Smiling or not smiling—
both have ended now.
Being ended or not being ended—
both have ended now.
You talk like a fool.

Your eyes, sister, are said to be
nothing but the four elements,
but they radiate love.
To be or not to be?
Why did you climb up the tree
in order to learn the fear of falling down?
Why ask the question

for confusion to be born
and life obstructed?

Your eyes, brother, are said to be
nothing but the four elements,
but they are flooded with the suffering of injustice.
My hands are here,
hoping that the water of compassion
will wash away that unjust mountain.

That gun is not to be blamed.
That hand is not to be blamed.
That bullet and that flower!
The plants are nurtured so that flowers bloom.
There are thorns to hurt you.
There are caterpillars that eat up the young stems,
caterpillars the color of emerald.
Your crystal clear tears
are of the same nature
as the drops of muddy water
on the roots of these plants.
What can I say?
Laughing sounds dumb.
Crying also sounds dumb.
Not laughing and not crying still sound dumb.
Laughing, laughing, crying, crying
more flowers should bloom for life.

In the world of men,
flowers are authentically flowers.
The flowers of thoughts
embrace time and space,

transcend the two extremes,
transcend matter and speed,
transcend matter and transformation.

O the smile of awakening
O the smile of strangeness
O the smile of persuasion
O the smile of great compassion.

In 1966, I toured Europe to speak out for peace in Vietnam. One afternoon in London, I visited the British Museum. I was impressed to see a fossilized body from the time of 3,000 years before Christ. The body was lying on its left side with its knees folded up against its chest. The whole body was intact—hair, nails—because the hot sand had preserved it. I was with a nine-year-old British girl, who was horrified to see the preserved body. She pulled on my sleeve and asked, "Will that happen to me?" I said, "No. It will not happen to you." I lied about something that Channa, the Buddha's charioteer, did not lie about to Siddhartha.

A few weeks later, in Paris, I woke up one night feeling my body to see whether I had been transformed into stone. It was two o'clock in the morning, and I sat up. After sitting for an hour, I felt like water raining on a mountain, washing, washing. I enjoyed sitting another hour in that position. Finally, I got up and wrote this poem in one stroke. The feeling and the images flowed so vigorously that they had a hard time coming out, like a big container overturned, with the water pushing its way out.

GETTING INTO THE STREAM

Each monk has a corner of the mat,
a place to sit
for meditation.
There, monk, sit still on it.
The spinning Earth carries us along.
The place you sit on is like a second-class seat on a train.
The monk will eventually get off at his station,
and his place will be dusted for someone else.

How long is the monk to sit
on his corner of the mat?
Sit still on it anyway.
Don't sit as if you will never give it up,
as if there is no station to arrive at.
The engine with its flames
will carry you along.

Each monk will sit in the lotus position
on the corner of the mat.
The monk will sit like an ancient, enormous mountain.
The mountain is there, completely still,
but like the monk it is on the turning Earth.
Unslowed by our fear,
this train of ours,
this fire-filled engine,
is hurrying ahead.

This morning,
the monk sits as usual
on his corner of the mat.

But he smiles.
"I will not sit here forever," he tells himself.
"When the train arrives at the station,
I will be elsewhere.
A corner of the mat
or an armful of grass—
I am sitting down
just one more time."

The fruits of the spiritual life, or meditation, are of four kinds. If you enter the stream, you know that soon you will arrive, because the stream is going to the ocean. You are called a "Stream Enterer." The second fruit is called "Once-Returner." You only have to return one more time. The third fruit is "Never-Returner." You will attain liberation in this life. The fourth fruit is "Arhat." You are completely liberated from the cycle of birth and death.

In Buddhist monasteries, twice a month novices recite a text by Master Qui Shan called Exhortation to Practitioners. *The monks are urged to practice diligently, because life is short and we cannot get hold of time. Each evening during our recitation, we chant, "Today has passed. Life has diminished. It's like a fish finding the level of water lower and lower. The community should work hard for deliverance."*

There are a few monks who thought that this poem was an attack on them. That is not true. This was written with great pain and compassion.

"An armful of grass" is what the Buddha needed before his enlightenment. He had tried many ascetic methods but didn't succeed. Asceticism is not the way. It is an extreme, like other extremes. The Buddha decided to break his fast. He drank some milk and ate some rice and felt fresh again. He had the impression that he only needed to make a final effort to have a breakthrough. He cut some fresh, green kusha grass, prepared his seat, and told himself with much determination, "I will sit down one more time. Until I 'get it,' I will not stand up." And he got enlightened.

I WILL SAY I WANT IT ALL

If you ask how much do I want,
I'll tell you that I want it all.
This morning, you and I
and all men
are flowing into the marvelous stream
of oneness.

Small pieces of imagination as we are,
we have come a long way to find ourselves
and for ourselves, in the dark, the illusion of emancipation.

This morning, my brother is back from his long adventure.
He kneels before the altar,
his eyes full of tears.
His soul is longing for a shore to set anchor at
(a yearning I once had).
Let him kneel there and weep.
Let him cry his heart out.
Let him have his refuge there for a thousand years,
enough to dry all his tears.

One night, I will come
and set fire to his shelter, the small cottage on the hill.
My fire will destroy everything
and remove his only life raft after a shipwreck.

In the utmost anguish of his soul,
the shell will break.
The light of the burning hut will witness
his glorious deliverance.

I will wait for him
beside the burning cottage.
Tears will run down my cheeks.
I will be there to contemplate his new being.
And as I hold his hands in mine
and ask him how much he wants,
he will smile and say that he wants it all—just as I did.

This is an old poem, written back in 1954. Someone who suffers a great deal might need to hide himself for a while. It is fine to hide oneself for some time for healing. But there are people who want to hide themselves for a long time, like those practitioners who hide themselves in the sitting. They need someone to come and burn down their hiding places.

ZEN CORNERS

There is only one zen center,
but there may be many zen corners.

Never mind.
A corner is a center,
and a center is not other than a corner.

Everywhere we chant, "Form is emptiness.
Form is not other than emptiness."

FROGLESSNESS

The first fruition of the practice
is the attainment of froglessness.

When a frog is put
on the center of a plate,
she will jump out of the plate
after just a few seconds.

If you put the frog back again
on the center of the plate,
she will again jump out.

You have so many plans.
There is something you want to become.
Therefore you always want to make a leap,
a leap forward.

It is difficult
to keep the frog still
on the center of the plate.
You and I
both have Buddha Nature in us.
This is encouraging,
but you and I
both have Frog Nature in us.

That is why
the first attainment
of the practice—
froglessness is its name.

GOING IN CIRCLES

O you who are going in circles,
please stop.
What are you doing it for?

"I cannot be without going,
because I don't know where to go.
That's why I go in circles."

O you who are going in circles,
please stop.

"But if I stop going,
I will stop being."

O my friend who is going in circles,
you are not one with
this crazy business of going in circles.
You may enjoy going,
but not going in circles.

"Where can I go?"

Go where you can find your beloved,
where you can find yourself.

TWENTY-FOUR BRAND-NEW HOURS

Waking up this morning, I see the blue sky.
I join my hands in thanks
for the many wonders of life;
for having twenty-four brand-new hours before me.
The sun is rising.
The forest becomes my awareness
bathed in the sunshine.

I walk across a field of sunflowers.
Tens of thousands of flowers are turned toward the bright east.
My awareness is like the sun.
My hands are sowing seeds for the next harvest.
My ear is filled with the sound of the rising tide.
In the magnificent sky, clouds are approaching
with joy from many directions.
I can see the fragrant lotus ponds of my homeland.
I can see coconut trees along the rivers.
I can see rice fields stretching, stretching,
laughing at the sun and rain.
Mother Earth gives us coriander, basil, celery, and mint.
Tomorrow the hills and mountains of the country
will be green again.
Tomorrow the buds of life will spring up quickly.
Folk poetry will be as sweet as the songs of children.

This is a song I wrote in Tokyo in 1970. It was meant to be included in the
first edition of The Miracle of Mindfulness *as "My Awareness, the Sun-*
shine." Sister Chân Không sings this on the tape Songs of Vietnam.

RENAISSANCE

This morning, at sunrise, a new bud appeared on the tree. It was born around midnight. The bark, the skin of the tree, split open under the incessant movement of its sap to make room for another life. However, the tree was not listening, was not feeling those movements, that pain. All it did was listen attentively to the whispering of the flowers and grasses that surrounded it. The fragrance of the night was pure and wondrous. The tree had no idea of passing time, of birth and death. It was there, as present as the sky and the earth.

This morning at dawn, I understand that this new day does not resemble any other, that this morning is unique. We often think that we store away certain mornings for later. But it is impossible. Each morning is special, unique. My friend, how do you find this morning? Is it here for the first time in our lives? Is it the repetition of a past morning? My friend, when we are not present, mornings repeat themselves. If we are present in front of life, each morning is a new space, a new time. The sun shines over different vistas, at different moments. Your full awareness is like the moon that bathes in the heart of hundreds of rivers: the river flows, the water sings, the moon travels under the immense dome of the blue sky. Look at that blue color, smile, and let your awareness spring up like the transparent, pure sunlight that caresses the branches and leaves in the early morning.

A morning is not a page that you cover with words and turn over at any moment. A book is a path where one can come and go. A morning is not a path, not even a path followed by a bird that flies away without leaving a trace. A morning is a symphony; for it to be there or not depends on your presence.

The new bud on the tree is not even a year old. It is the bud of mindfulness and deep looking that, at each moment, in perpetual motion, opens up to life. If you see the new bud, you will be able to go beyond the limits of time, for true life is beyond months, beyond years.

Your eyes are the immense sky, the high mountain, the deep ocean. Your life does not know borders. All the delicious fruit and magnificent flowers belong to you. Accept them . . .

THE RAINBOW CHILDREN

I was awake,
yet the dream continued.
Fascinated, I saw myself inside a museum
where all the memories of my childhood were on display.

The moon of a wild land
filtering through the bamboo bars of the window
plunged the young man into a deep sleep,
where the dream continued,
the thread of water
on a serene autumn lake.

My friend, why offer a poem to a singing bird,
to a pebble in a clear stream,
to a fish swimming freely?

What a magnificent morning
on this clear, blue planet!
At this very moment when the multitude of stars
melts into the celestial dome,
children,
children by the thousands,
children of all colors,
climb up the mountain
and look down below, with utmost attention.
They are watching me.

But I keep on sleeping.
Without opening my eyes,
I stretch my body peacefully

and wait for the surprise to arrive!
Why offer a poem
to the little hut
hidden in the bamboo thicket,
to the sunflower unfurled against the wall,
to the sleeping dog curled in a ball in the courtyard
to the cat dancing with sunbeams
high upon the haystack?

Daybreak
does not resemble a new page in a book.
It is a symphony to rebirth,
with its full array of sounds and colors.
Each dawn is an ode
to twenty-four brand-new hours.

[UNTITLED]

Clouds softly pillow the mountain peak.
The breeze is fragrant with tea blossoms.
The joy of meditation remains unshakable.
The forest offers floral perfumes.
One morning we awaken,
fog wrapped around the roof.
With fresh laughter, we bid farewell.
The musical clamor of birds
sends us back on the ten thousand paths,
to watch a dream as generous as the sea.
A flicker of fire from the familiar stove
warms the evening shadows as they fall.
Impermanent, self-emptied life,
filled with impostors whose sweet speech
hides a wicked heart.
My confidence intact,
I bid farewell with a peaceful heart.
The affairs of this world are merely a dream.
Don't forget that days and months race by
as quickly as a young horse.
The stream of birth and death dissolves,
but our friendship never disappears.

OUR TRUE HERITAGE

The cosmos is filled with precious gems.
I want to offer a handful of them to you this morning.
Each moment you are alive is a gem,
shining through and containing earth and sky,
water and clouds.

It needs you to breathe gently
for the miracles to be displayed.
Suddenly you hear the birds singing,
the pines chanting,
see the flowers blooming,
the blue sky,
the white clouds,
the smile and the marvelous look
of your beloved.

You, the richest person on Earth,
who have been going around begging for a living,
stop being the destitute child.
Come back and claim your heritage.
We should enjoy our happiness
and offer it to everyone.
Cherish this very moment.
Let go of the stream of distress
and embrace life fully in your arms.

These are the words of a song written during the Winter 1990 retreat at Plum Village, inspired by the parable of the destitute son in the Lotus Sutra *and also the idea of generosity in the* Diamond Sutra.

THE GOOD NEWS

They don't publish
the good news.
The good news is published
by us.
We have a special edition every moment,
and we need you to read it.
The good news is that you are alive,
and the linden tree is still there,
standing firm in the harsh winter.
The good news is that you have wonderful eyes
to touch the blue sky.
The good news is that your child is there before you,
and your arms are available:
hugging is possible.
They only print what is wrong.
Look at each of our special editions.
We always offer the things that are not wrong.
We want you to benefit from them
and help protect them.
The dandelion is there by the sidewalk,
smiling its wondrous smile,
singing the song of eternity.
Listen! You have ears that can hear it.
Bow your head.
Listen to it.
Leave behind the world of sorrow
and preoccupation
and get free.
The latest good news
is that you can do it.

Plum Village, March 1992.

BHUMISPARSHA

Death comes
with his impressive scythe
and says,
"You should be afraid of me."
I look up and ask,
"Why should I be afraid of you?"
"Because I will make you dead.
I will make you nonexistent."
"How can you make me nonexistent?"

Death does not answer.
He swings his impressive scythe.

I say, "I come and I go. Then I come again. And I go again.
I always come back. You can neither make me exist nor nonexist."
"How do you know that you will come again?" Death asks.
"I know because I have done that countless times," I say.
"How do I know that you are telling the truth?
Who can be the witness?" Death frowns.

I touch the Earth and say,
"Earth is the witness. She is my mother."

Suddenly, Death hears the music.
Suddenly, Death hears the birds singing from all directions.
Suddenly, Death sees the trees blossoming.
Earth makes herself apparent to Death
and smiles lovingly to him.
Death melts in the loving gaze of Earth.

O my beloved,
touch Earth every time you get scared.
Touch her deeply,
and your sorrow will melt away.
Touch her deeply,
and you will touch the Deathless.

REFUGE PRAYER

At the foot of the Bodhi tree,
beautifully seated, peaceful and smiling,
the living source of understanding and compassion,
to the Buddha I go for refuge.

The path of mindful living,
leading to healing, joy, and enlightenment,
the way of peace,
to the Dharma I go for refuge.

The loving and supportive community of practice,
realizing harmony, awareness, and liberation,
to the Sangha I go for refuge.

I am aware that the Three Gems are within my heart.
I vow to realize them.
I vow to practice mindful breathing and smiling,
looking deeply into things.
I vow to understand living beings and their suffering,
to cultivate compassion and loving kindness,
and to practice joy and equanimity.

I vow to offer joy to one person in the morning
and to help relieve the grief of one person in the afternoon.
I vow to live simply and sanely,
content with just a few possessions,
and to keep my body healthy.
I vow to let go of all worry and anxiety
in order to be light and free.

I am aware that I owe so much to my parents, teachers, friends,
   and all beings.
I vow to be worthy of their trust,
to practice wholeheartedly,
so that understanding and compassion will flower,
and I can help living beings
be free from their suffering.

May the Buddha, the Dharma, and the Sangha support my
   efforts.

TAKING REFUGE

Breathing in, I go back
to the island within myself.
There are beautiful trees
within the island.
There are clear streams of water.
There are birds,
sunshine,
and fresh air.
Breathing out,
I feel safe.
I enjoy going back to my island.

Breathing in mindfully,
I meet the Buddha within myself.
Buddha is mindfulness.
His torch is always there
illuminating my path,
the path of coming,
the path of going,
the path of my mind,
the path of my life.
Breathing out mindfully,
I see my path clearly,
far or near.

Breathing in,
I find the Dharma in my breath.
The breathing protects me,
protects my body,
protects my spirit.

Breathing out,
I keep the breath alive
for my continual protection.

Breathing in,
I recognize the five skandhas
as my Sangha.
The breathing establishes harmony.
The breathing generates peace.
Breathing out, I enjoy the Oneness
of my being.

[UNTITLED]

Walking joyfully in the ultimate dimension,
walk with your feet,
not with your head.
If you walk with your head, you'll get lost.

Teaching the Dharma in the ultimate dimension,
falling leaves fill the sky.
The path is covered with autumn moonlight.
The Dharma is neither full nor empty.

Discussing the Dharma in the ultimate dimension,
we look at each other and smile.
You are me, don't you see?
Speaking and listening are one.

Enjoying lunch in the historical dimension,
I feed all generations of ancestors
and all future generations.
Together, we will find our way.

Getting angry in the historical dimension,
we close our eyes and look deeply.
Where will we be in three hundred years?
We open our eyes and hug.

Resting in the ultimate dimension,
using snowy mountains as a pillow
and pink clouds as blankets,
we become sky and earth.

Meditating in the ultimate dimension,
Every moment is a realization.
Every tree is a Bodhi tree.
Every seat is Prabhutaratna's lion seat.

WALKING MEDITATION

Take my hand.
We will walk.
We will only walk.
We will enjoy our walk
without thinking of arriving anywhere.
Walk peacefully.
Walk happily.
Our walk is a peace walk.
Our walk is a happiness walk.

Then we learn
that there is no peace walk;
that peace is the walk;
that there is no happiness walk;
that happiness is the walk.
We walk for ourselves.
We walk for everyone
always hand in hand.

Walk and touch peace every moment.
Walk and touch happiness every moment.
Each step brings a fresh breeze.
Each step makes a flower bloom under our feet.
Kiss the Earth with your feet.
Print on Earth your love and happiness.

Earth will be safe
when we feel in us enough safety.

EACH STEP

Through the deserted gate,
full of ripened leaves,
I follow the small path.
Earth is as red as a child's lips.
Suddenly
l am aware
of each step
I make.

CUCKOO TELEPHONE

The cuckoos have not missed their appointment.
Rolling hills are growing warm.
The telephone is ringing loudly from hill to hill.
The gentle spring rain permeates the soil of my consciousness.
A seed that has lain deeply in the Earth for many years
just smiles.

You just came for a visit.
Your travel bag is half full of moonlight.
The spinach leaf is calling for the seed of basilicum.
There is more green than red now.
The vegetation is luxurious.
The bell is calling.
Our feet kiss the Earth.
Our eyes embrace the Sky.
We walk in mindfulness.

Ten thousand lives can be seen in a single instant.
This is still springtime,
when everything is manifesting itself
so rapidly.
The snow is green.
And the sunshine is falling like the rain.

Every time I leave Plum Village for a spring teaching tour, I remind my friends that when spring comes, the sound of the cuckoos is my telephone call. And as we always practice telephone meditation in Plum Village, practicing conscious breathing when the telephone bell rings, my friends always stop and breathe deeply when they hear the cuckoos.

A friend who visits you without some moonlight in his or her traveling bag is too busy. When you see such a friend, ask him or her, "Do you have enough moonlight in your bag?" That would be a bell of mindfulness.

As you look at the luxurious vegetation in spring, you know the snow that fell in the winter is part of what you see. You can see the snow that wears a green coat. It was the sunshine that helped bring the ocean water up to the sky in the form of clouds, so the sunshine can be seen in the rain or the snow that is falling. Since the snow is falling, you see the sunshine fall as well.

EARTH TOUCHING

Here is the foot of a tree.
Here is an empty, quiet place.
Here is a cushion.
Brother, why don't you sit down?

Sit upright.
Sit with solidity.
Sit in peace.
Don't let your thoughts lift you up into the air.
Sit so that you can really touch the Earth
and be one with her.
You may like to smile, brother.
Earth will transmit to you her solidity,
her peace, and her joy.
With your mindful breathing,
with your peaceful smile,
you sustain the mudra of Earth Touching.

There were times when you didn't do well.
Sitting on Earth, but it was as if you were floating in the air,
you who used to go in circles in the triple world
and be drawn into the ocean of illusion.
But Earth is always patient
and one-hearted.
Earth is still waiting for you
because Earth has been waiting for you
during the last trillion lives.
That is why she can wait for you for any other length of time.
She knows that finally you will come back to her one day.
She will welcome you

always fresh and green, exactly like the first time,
because love never says, "This is the last";
because Earth is a loving mother.
She will never stop waiting for you.

Do go back to her, brother.
You will be like that tree.
The leaves, the branches, and the flowers of your soul
will be fresh and green
once you enter the mudra of Earth Touching.

The empty path welcomes you, sister,
fragrant with grass and little flowers,
the path paved with paddy fields
still bearing the marks of your childhood
and the fragrance of mother's hand.
Walk leisurely, peacefully.
Your feet should deeply touch the Earth.
Don't let your thoughts lift you up into the air, sister.
Go back to the path every moment.
The path is your dearest friend.
She will transmit to you
her solidity,
her peace.

With your deep breathing,
you sustain the mudra of Earth Touching.
Walk as if you were kissing the Earth with your feet,
as if you were massaging the Earth.
The marks left by your feet
will be like the marks of an emperor's seal
calling for Now to go back to Here;

so that life will be present;
so that the blood will bring the color of love to your face;
so that the wonders of life will be manifested,
and all afflictions will be transformed into
peace and joy.

There were times when you did not succeed, sister.
Walking on the empty path, but you were floating in the air,
because you used to get lost in samsara
and drawn into the world of illusion.
But the beautiful path is always patient.
It is always waiting for you to come back,
that path which is so familiar to you,
that path which is so faithful.
It knows deeply that you will come back one day.
It will be joyful to welcome you back.
It will be as fresh and as beautiful as the first time.
Love never says, "This is the last."

That path is you, sister.
That is why it will never be tired of waiting.
Whether it is covered now with red dust
or with autumn leaves
or icy snow—
do go back to the path, sister,
because I know
you will be like that tree,
the leaves, the trunk, the branches,
and the blossoms of your soul
will be fresh and beautiful,
once you enter the mudra of Earth Touching.

BREATHING

Breathing in,
I see myself as a flower.
I am the freshness
of a dewdrop.
Breathing out,
my eyes have become flowers.
Please look at me.
l am looking
with the eyes of love.

Breathing in,
I am a mountain,
imperturbable,
still,
alive,
vigorous.
Breathing out,
I feel solid.
The waves of emotion
can never carry me away.

Breathing in,
I am still water.
I reflect the sky
faithfully.
Look, I have a full moon
within my heart,
the refreshing moon of the bodhisattva.
Breathing out,

I offer the perfect reflection
of my mirror-mind.

Breathing in,
I have become space
without boundaries.
I have no plans left.
I have no luggage.
Breathing out,
I am the moon
that is sailing through the sky of utmost emptiness.
I am freedom.

OPEN THE ROAD WIDER

Hair which is the color of precious wood
is now offered as incense.
Beauty becomes eternity.
How wonderful the awareness of impermanence!

Since everything is as a dream,
the true mind is determined to lead the way.
After listening to the voice of the rising tide,
steps are made in the direction of the unconditioned.

The winds chant this morning on the slope of Gridhrakuta.
The mind is no longer bound to anything.
The song now is that of the lovely teaching;
its fragrance is the essence of truth.

In times past, it was with *boket* water
that her hair was washed,
then dried in the fragrant breeze of the late afternoon.
This morning it is the bodhi nectar that she receives
for the mind of enlightenment to appear in its wholeness.

For twenty-five years
she has made daily offerings
of loving kindness with her hands.
Compassion has never ceased to grow in her heart.

This morning her hair is shed,
and the Way becomes wide open.
Suffering and illusion, though limitless,
are entirely ended.

A heart can touch the ten directions.

*This poem was written for Sister Chân Không the day she shed her hair on
the Gridhrakuta Mountain to become a nun.*

ALSO BY THICH NHAT HANH

ABOUT THICH NHAT HANH

THICH NHAT HANH was a world-renowned spiritual teacher and peace activist. Born in Vietnam in 1926, he became a Zen Buddhist monk at the age of sixteen. Over seven decades of teaching, he published more than 100 books, which have sold more than four million copies in the United States alone. Exiled from Vietnam in 1966 for promoting peace, his teachings on Buddhism as a path to social and political transformation are responsible for bringing the mindfulness movement to Western culture. He established the international Plum Village Community of Engaged Buddhism in France, now the largest Buddhist monastery in Europe and the heart of a growing community of mindfulness practice centers around the world. He passed away in 2022 at the age of ninety-five at his root temple, Tu Hieu, in Hue, Vietnam.

Monastics and visitors practice the art of mindful living in the tradition of Thich Nhat Hanh at our mindfulness practice centers around the world. To reach any of these communities, or for information about how individuals, couples, and families can join in a retreat, please contact:

PLUM VILLAGE
33580 Dieulivol, France
plumvillage.org

LA MAISON DE L'INSPIR
77510 Villeneuve-sur-Bellot, France
maisondelinspir.org

HEALING SPRING
MONASTERY
77510 Verdelot, France
healingspringmonastery.org

MAGNOLIA GROVE
MONASTERY
Batesville, MS 38606, USA
magnoliagrovemonastery.org

BLUE CLIFF MONASTERY
Pine Bush, NY 12566, USA
bluecliffmonastery.org

DEER PARK MONASTERY
Escondido, CA 92026, USA
deerparkmonastery.org

EUROPEAN INSTITUTE OF
APPLIED BUDDHISM
D-51545 Waldbröl, Germany
eiab.eu

THAILAND PLUM VILLAGE
Nakhon Ratchasima
30130 Thailand
thaiplumvillage.org

ASIAN INSTITUTE OF
APPLIED BUDDHISM
Lantau Island, Hong Kong
pvfhk.org

STREAM ENTERING
MONASTERY
Beaufort, Victoria 3373
Australia
nhapluu.org

MOUNTAIN SPRING
MONASTERY
Bilpin, NSW 2758, Australia
mountainspringmonastery.org

For more information visit: *plumvillage.org*
To find an online sangha visit: *plumline.org*
For more resources, try the Plum Village app: *plumvillage.app*
Social media: *@thichnhathanh @plumvillagefrance*

Parallax Press, a nonprofit publisher founded by Zen Master Thich Nhat Hanh, publishes books and media on the art of mindful living and Engaged Buddhism. We are committed to offering teachings that help transform suffering and injustice. Our aspiration is to contribute to collective insight and awakening, bringing about a more joyful, healthy, and compassionate society.

View our entire library at **parallax.org**.